To Pamela, Happy Cooking!
Terry.
4th May 1999

*A selection of
personal recipes and
stories by Terry Farr*

Text © Terry Farr
Friends Restaurant 1998

Terry Farr has asserted his moral
right to be identified as the Author
of this work.

All rights reserved. No part of this
publication may be stored in a
retrieval system, or transmitted
in any form or by any means,
electronic, mechanical or otherwise, without prior permission of
the copyright holder.

First published in 1998
by Terry Farr

ISBN 0 9534777 0 3

Designed by Lynn Oxford
Edited by Donald Lyon
Photographs by Terry Farr

Printed and bound in Great Britain
by Burlington Press, Station Road,
Foxton, Cambridge CB2 6SW.

Contents

4	Foreword
5	Introduction
6	Conversion Tables
8	Terrine of Seafish with Hot Chive Sauce
9	Breast of Pigeon Sautéed with Spinach & Lardons
10	Grilled Salmon with Roasted Red Peppers & Watercress Sauce
11	Venison Stew with Spätzle
12	Honey & Whisky Délice
13	Lemon Pudding Soufflé
15	Courgette Soufflé
16	Smoked Salmon Pancakes with Cream & Chives
17	Poached Chicken Breast with Vegetables & Herbs
20	Galette of Aubergines, Tomatoes & Mozzarella
21	Grape Tart
24	Hot Date & Banana Pudding
28	Asparagus wrapped in Smoked Salmon baked in Wafer-Thin Pastry
29	Salmon Fishcakes
32	Calves' Liver with Bubble & Squeak & Onion Gravy
33	Fillet of Beef with Caramelised Shallots, Wild Mushrooms & Red Wine
34	Prune & Armagnac Tart
35	Chocolate Soufflé
37	Marinated Salmon
38	Caramelised Onion & Emmental Tartlet
39	Polenta with Mushrooms & Herbs
40	Confit of Duck with Garlic Mash
41	Chocolate Marquise
42	Pear & Almond Tart
44	Duck Livers with Balsamic Vinegar & Almonds
45	Bulwinkle's Mackerel Brandade
46	Guinea Fowl with Yellow Pepper Coulis
47	Salmon Baked in Filo Pastry
48	Orange Bread & Butter Pudding
49	Apple & Calvados Tart
53	Rillettes of Duck
56	Watercress Soup with Salmon Dumplings
57	Jambonneau of Chicken
60	Roast Monkfish with Garlic & Wild Mushrooms
61	Rhubarb Tart Brulée
64	Coconut Parfait with Pineapple Compote
66	Crab Cakes with Grain Mustard
67	Avocado & Smoked Chicken with Poppy Seed Dressing
68	Grilled Tuna with Béarnaise Sauce
69	Noisettes of Pork with Ginger & Spring Onion
70	Raspberry Mille-Feuille
71	White Chocolate Bavarois
73	Goats' Cheese & Red Pepper Tart
74	Soused Herrings
75	Chicken Cooked in Ratatouille
76	Vegetable Strudel
77	Victoria Plum & Amaretti Tart with Blackberry Coulis
78	Strawberry Délice
80	Green Bean & Tarragon Soup
81	Crabmeat Sausage with Grain Mustard & Brioche Crumb
84	Wild Boar Medallions & Rösti
85	Halibut in Vermouth with Black Noodles
88	Summer Pudding
89	Clafoutis aux Cerises
93	Terrine of Lobster & Sole with Pistachio Nuts
96	Hot Vichyssoise with Smoked Salmon & Chives
97	Partridge Pudding
98	Sea Bass with Caramelised Fennel
99	Hazelnut Meringue Gateau
100	Warm Fig & Wild Honey Tart
102	Kipper Pâté with Whisky
103	Grilled Goats' Cheese with Celery & Walnuts
104	Spinach Gnocchi (Gnocchi Verde)
105	Salmis of Wild Duck
106	Lime Tart
107	Butterscotch Brulée
109	Jerusalem Artichoke Soup
110	Scallops & Bacon with Honey & Sesame
111	Roast Suprême of Pheasant "Grande-Mere"
112	Roast Loin of Lamb Stuffed with Dried Exotic Fruits
113	Honey & Walnut Flan
114	Chestnut Charlotte
115-116	Basic Recipes - Sauces
117-120	Basic Recipes - Stocks
121-126	Basic Recipes - Pastry
127	Glossary

Foreword

By David Suchet

I have lived in Pinner for ten years now. It is an ancient coaching village which still maintains its character in spite of having been geographically absorbed into the metropolitan sprawl.

Since Friends Restaurant was taken over here in the High Street six years ago, I have been a regular visitor and was delighted when Terry Farr asked me to write the foreword for his book of recipes.

Friends Restaurant has prospered during those six years, enjoying consecutive entries in the Michelin and AA guides. And Terry himself has been honoured with membership of the élite Master Chefs of Great Britain.

In my hectic schedule, I enjoy the quiet escape to the old world charm of 'Friends', a warm convivial atmosphere, superb dishes, constantly changing menus and the excellent service. It is indeed a favourite haunt for my wife and I.

I am grateful to Terry for the many ways he has supported the local community here. I heartily endorse what he is doing here at Friends, and I wish him and his team - Head Chef Ben Denny and Restaurant Manager Alex Pathak - every success for their future in Pinner.

Introduction

By Terry Farr, November 1998

Ever since I started my career in cookery, I have wanted to share my ideas with people. Food inspires a perpetual enthusiasm in me, and I just can't keep it to myself. I have to pass it on. I have enjoyed many fruitful relationships with people who share that enthusiasm, notably those who now spend much of their lives in the kitchen at Friends.

Quite often, however, I have found that I am not getting through. Certain people's eyes tend to glaze over when I start to go on about my obsession. Well, I don't mind. After all, many people have other interests (I can't begin to think what they might be, but they tell me they have) and they simply haven't got time to stop and listen to me going on about my particular addiction.

That is why I have decided to write a book. It seems to me to be the perfect solution. I can communicate my ideas, and people can then decide whether to take them or leave them. That way we're all happy! So here it is. My first book. It is the culmination of years of preparation, and it would not have been possible without a little help from a few Friends.

Specifically, I am indebted to the varied artistic talents of Lynn Oxford, and her gentle cajoling and encouragement during the times when it looked as though things were never going to get finished. Thanks are also due to Donald Lyon for his tirelessly creative penmanship, both on this project and generally over recent years.

Without Friends Restaurant, there would be no book. And there would be no Friends Restaurant without a team that I have come to rely on for dedication above and beyond the call of duty. Alex, Ben, Simon, Judith and Sean, I thank you all for your enthusiasm for this project and for your tolerance in dodging camera equipment whilst continuing to serve happy customers!

And again, without those happy customers, Friends Restaurant would not exist. I am grateful to all of you who have come to eat at our tables over the past six years, and sincerely hope that we shall have the opportunity of entertaining you again in the future.

A special thank you must go to David Suchet, in my opinion the greatest character actor of his generation, for taking time out from his busy schedule to write the foreword to this book.

And finally, to the ones who always get a raw deal in introductions, the family. Jo, my wife, and my sons, Ben and Jamie, know that they are the number one passion in my life. And they have my everlasting gratitude for allowing me to indulge my other great passion: FOOD!

Conversion Tables

Weights Imperial | **Approximate Metric Equivalent**

Imperial	Metric
¼ oz	5 g
½ oz	10 g
¾ oz	20 g
1 oz	25 g
1½ oz	40 g
2 oz	50 g
2½ oz	60 g
3 oz	75 g
4 oz	110 g
4½ oz	125 g
5 oz	150 g
6 oz	175 g
7 oz	200 g
8 oz	225 g
9 oz	250 g
10 oz	275 g
11 oz	300 g
12 oz	350 g
13 oz	375 g
14 oz	400 g
15 oz	425 g
16 oz	450 g
1½ lb	700 g
2 lb	900 g
3 lb	1.35 kg

Fluid Measure

Imperial	Metric
2 fl oz	55 ml
3 fl oz	75 ml
4 fl oz	110 ml
5 fl oz (¼ pt)	150 ml
½ pt	275 ml
¾ pt	425 ml
1 pt	570 ml
1¼ pt	725 ml
1½ pt	900 ml
1¾ pt	1 l
2 pt	1.2 l
2½ pt	1.5 l
3 pt	1.7 l
4 pt	2.25 l

The weight measures above will also roughly suffice for conversion of fl oz to ml eg. 8 fl oz is roughly 225ml.

Measurements

Imperial	Metric
⅛ in	3 mm
¼ in	5 mm
½ in	1 cm
¾ in	2 cm
1 in	2.5 cm
1¼ in	3 cm
1½ in	4 cm
1¾ in	4.5 cm
2 in	5 cm
1½ in	6 cm
3 in	7.5 cm
3½ in	9 cm
4 in	10 cm
5 in	13 cm
5½ in	13.5 cm
6 in	15 cm
6½ in	16 cm
7 in	18 cm
7½ in	19 cm
8 in	20 cm
9 in	23 cm
9½ in	24 cm
10 in	25.5 cm
11 in	28 cm
12 in	30 cm

Oven Temperature Chart

Description	C	Gas mark	F
Low, Slow, Cool	110	¼	225
	120	½	250
	140	1	275
	150	2	300
	170	3	325
Moderate, Medium	180	4	350
	190	5	375
	200	6	400
Hot	220	7	425
	230	8	450
	240	9	475

January

Each recipe in this book has a story attached to it. And each month has a section of a larger story, about a little boy called Al who lived in the forest, and who was once privileged to meet all the months together at once.

The sequence of this book mirrors the procession of the months. But you could also say that this book lets you see all the months at once, just like Al did.

Al lived with his wicked stepmother (there's always a wicked stepmother in fairy stories like this one). It all started one freezing winter's night in January.

Terrine of Seafish with Hot Chive Sauce

The fresh taste of the sea with a velvety and colourful sauce

Serves 8-10

Ingredients:

    8 oz / 225 g Dover sole fillets
    8 oz / 225 g salmon fillets
    8 oz / 225 g sea bream fillets
       (make sure all pin bones are removed)
    2 egg whites
    6 fl oz / 175 ml double cream
    salt and Cayenne pepper
    1/2 pt / 275 ml beurre blanc (see page 115)
    2 tbsp chopped chives
    1/2 a lemon

Method:

The Terrine:

1. Line a 2 pt / 1.2 l terrine with clingfilm.

2. Blend half the sole with one egg white in a food processor until smooth, then turn out into a mixing bowl set in ice. Beat in half the cream and season lightly. Take half the salmon fillet and repeat the procedure.

3. Spread half the blended sole on the bottom of the lined terrine and lay the remaining salmon fillet evenly on top of this. Spread the remainder of the blended sole evenly over the salmon.

4. Lay the bream fillets evenly on top of the sole, and spread half the blended salmon over the bream.

5. Lay the sole fillets evenly on top, then cover with the remaining blended salmon. Overlap the clingfilm so that the contents of the terrine are covered. Cover with a layer of foil and put the lid on.

6. Cook the terrine in a bain-Marie (a roasting tray half filled with water) at Gas 5 / 375°F / 190°C for 55 minutes. Test to see if it is cooked by inserting a thin-bladed knife. If it is clean on withdrawal, the terrine is ready.

The Chive Sauce:

1. Warm the beurre blanc (see page 115), and add the chopped chives. Add a few drops of lemon juice, and a little seasoning to taste.

2. Turn the terrine out onto a serving dish, remove the clingfilm, and slice onto warm plates as required. Serve the chive sauce separately, or in a cordon poured around the slices, if you prefer.

Schoolboys can be cruel. But so can schoolmasters. I was once taught by a failed army officer who had decided to take up drilling classes of schoolboys instead of squaddies.

One day our class held a council of war. We would each play a small trick on this master. We ran through the usual gamut of schoolboy tricks. Tying shoelaces together, booby-trapping board rubbers, blackboards and chalk, and rigging chairs and desks to behave eccentrically.

But Oliver "Ferret" Frisby didn't seem to have a plan. Frankly he was a "swot", and the only boy in the class who usually escaped Mr Gudgeon's attentions.

But then Mr Gudgeon started having serious problems. He was in charge of school dinners, and people started complaining of a horrible smell in the dining room.

It was only at the end of term that a severely decayed fish was found nailed to the underside of one of the tables. When Oliver returned the next term he was given a hero's welcome!

Please don't follow Oliver's example. Only use the freshest of fish for this recipe!

Breast of Pigeon Sautéed with Spinach & Lardons

A succulent combination of game and moist, fresh spinach

Serves 4

Ingredients:

- 4 plump pigeon breasts, trimmed and skinned
- 6 oz / 175 g smoked streaky bacon, cut into lardons
- 1 1/2 lb / 700 g young spinach, washed and dried with stalks removed
- 5 fl oz / 150 ml port
- 2 sprigs fresh thyme
- 4 juniper berries, crushed
- 1 clove garlic, peeled and sliced
- 2 tbsp olive oil
- 2 oz / 50 g unsalted butter
- 5 fl oz / 150 ml Madeira

Method:

1. Place the pigeon breasts in the port together with the juniper, garlic and thyme for 2-3 hours.

2. Blanch the lardons in boiling water, then cook them in a little of the olive oil until lightly crisp. Reserve.

3. Remove the pigeon breasts from the marinade and season. Cook them in the remaining olive oil at a high temperature, leaving them pink in the middle.

4. Deglaze the pan with the Madeira, strain the juices and keep warm.

5. In a thick-bottomed pan, melt the butter until light brown (beurre noisette), then add the spinach. Season lightly and cook evenly for about 1 minute.

6. Place the spinach in the centres of 4 hot plates, carve the breasts into slices and arrange on top of the spinach.

7. Sprinkle the warm lardons over the tops of the dishes and drizzle the juices around. Serve immediately.

Early in my career, way back in the sixties, I worked in the kitchens at the Connaught. I remember this story as "The Mystery of the Short-Trousered Chef". (Sherlock Holmes would have been proud of me!)

The Chef Saucier, M. Delorme, was a real character. 65 years old, he always used to come to work with his trousers rolled half-way up his shins. In those days you had too much respect to make any comment. But curiosity got the better of me. Fearfully, I asked him the secret of his trousers.

"Young man" he answered, "at the end of service, you will have your answer."

I waited until it was time to go home. Then I studied M. Delorme's trousers once more. Sure enough, the exertions of kitchen life had had the same effect that building work seems to have on modern builders. That is, his waistband had slipped down several inches! The result was that his turnups now broke neatly over his shoes.

A loveable eccentric. He loved game recipes, and this one reminds me of him.

Grilled Salmon with Roasted Peppers & Watercress Sauce

A classic combination of colours and flavours

Visiting the Napa Valley of California once, I was looking forward to exploring the vineyards and their produce. Unfortunately, my hostess turned out to be a very big-hearted lady - who intended her big heart to stay healthy!

So I found myself one afternoon sitting in an immense puddle of sulphurous mud with slices of vegetable matter stuck to my eyes, enjoying the delights of a local health spa!

As if this were not bad enough, I couldn't think what to cook her for dinner. If so much as a molecule of full cream produce passed her lips I would be for it. I decided to make the best of a bad job and doze off.

As I drifted away, my skin went a soft shade of pink and crisped up delicately at the edges. And the sulphurous mud was actually very tasty natural yoghurt. Somebody had also swapped the boring slices of cucumber over my eyes for some rather decorative slices of assorted peppers.

When I awoke my recipe was all ready in my head. Things looked much better!

Serves 4

Ingredients:

- 4 x 5 oz / 150 g fillets of salmon
- 1 each of yellow, red and green peppers (deseeded and diced)
- 1 shallot and 1 clove garlic (finely chopped together)
- 1 tbsp extra virgin olive oil
- 16 small new potatoes (all the same size)
- 1 bunch watercress (washed)
- 1 tbsp natural yoghurt
- a few drops of lemon juice
- Salt and milled pepper

Method:

1. Blanch the watercress in lightly seasoned boiling water. Strain and liquidise and add the yoghurt. Season with salt and pepper and a few drops of lemon juice. Leave to cool and adjust consistency with a little water.

2. Heat a small roasting tray, add the olive oil and peppers, and roast in a hot oven for 5 minutes. Add the garlic and shallot mixture and roast for a further 2-3 minutes. Season with salt and pepper.

3. Cook the new potatoes in boiling water until tender and keep warm.

4. Season the fish and place it in a heated grill pan, presentation side downwards. Grill for 5 minutes, turn over, and grill for a further 5 minutes, or until just cooked.

5. To serve, take 4 hot plates, place peppers in the centre of each plate and a salmon fillet on top. Pour the sauce around the edge of the plates and garnish with new potatoes.

Venison Stew with Spätzle

A hearty stew with a rich gamey flavour

Serves 4

Ingredients:

For the Spätzle:
1 1/2 lb / 700 g plain flour
3 large eggs
a good pinch of salt
1/2 pt / 275 ml lukewarm water

For the Marinade:
1 onion, sliced
2 cloves garlic, smashed
1 bayleaf, 1 sprig of thyme
1/2 pt / 275 ml full-bodied red wine
3 juniper berries, smashed

For the Venison:
1 1/2 lb / 700 g venison, diced (shoulder is best for this recipe)
1/2 lb / 225 g streaky bacon, roughly chopped
2 oz / 50 g butter
2 oz / 50 g plain flour
2 medium sized onions
2 cloves garlic
8 fl oz / 225 ml Madeira wine
1 tbsp chives

Method:

The Venison:

1. Place the meat in the marinade and leave it overnight in the fridge.

2. Fry the bacon gently in the butter for 6-8 minutes. Remove the bacon and place to one side.

3. Remove the meat from the marinade and drain well. Season and add it to the hot fat. Colour the meat well at a high temperature then remove to a casserole.

4. Fry the onions and garlic until golden brown. Add the flour and cook gently for 5-8 minutes. Add the marinade gradually to the pan, stirring continuously. Add the Madeira and cook gently for 20-25 minutes.

5. Strain the sauce over the meat and cook in a moderate oven for 1 1/2-2 hours. Check seasoning.

The Spätzle:

1. First make a smooth dough, using a wooden spoon. Whisk the eggs and half the water together with the salt. Add the flour and the rest of the water little by little, alternating between the two and beating well.

2. Choose a pot over which a metal colander will fit. Fill the pot with salted water and bring to the boil.

3. Remove the pot from the heat and place the colander over the top. Put the dough in the colander a little at a time, and force through the holes with the back of a wooden spoon.

4. When you have squeezed all the dough through remove the colander and return the pan to the heat and bring back to the boil. The spätzle are ready as soon as they float to the surface of the boiling water.

5. Strain, toss in butter and serve on top of the finished dish, sprinkle with finely cut chives.

This is my Grandpa Hugo's eccentric method for spätzle, a traditional German garnish. Hugo had a penchant for Shakespeare. He would often quote with great Germanic gravity. But not the well-known passages. He had his own library of Shakespearean sayings that appealed to him.

One morning, he got ready to go out. I asked where he was going.

"Ach, Terry. There's a special providence in the fall of a sparrow, as the great Shakespeare says". With that, he picked up his gun and walked out into the woods, shaking his head gravely.

When he returned, he went to the kitchen and began cooking. He made a game stew with spätzle. Half way through our meal he said "Well, Terry, you agree with Shakespeare? The sparrows taste wonderful, no?"

I looked at my plate. "You didn't shoot sparrows, did you?", I asked.

He chuckled. "It depends what you mean by "sparrows". You see, the garnish is called spätzle, which means "little sparrow" in German!"

I don't know if the German reputation for humour is enhanced by this story or not!

Honey & Whisky Délice

A warming winter combination using whisky and oatmeal

I once stayed in a craggy old Highland hotel. One night I overheard the owner discussing the hotel's ghostly history with some spellbound American tourists:

"Ye might hear the 6th Earl doing his rounds during the night. The puir man was very partial to a wee drop o' whisky in his porridge. One morning there was not a dram in the house. He set off to buy some in his slippers and dressing-gown, in a raging blizzard, without bothering to shut the front door!"

"Days later they dug him out of his snow-hole, stone cold. From the empty bottle with him, they knew he hadna' been stone cold sober when he died!" then she stamped her foot. "And to this day" she shouted angrily, "he nivver shuts the door after him!"

Somewhere off in the silence a heavy door banged shut.

"Thank you", she breathed.

The Americans were spellbound. But I am more inclined to put my faith in the dry Scots sense of humour. Our hostess had a particularly individual way of warning her staff to "shut that door!"

Serves 4

Ingredients:

For the Bavarois:
1/2 pt / 275 ml double cream
2 eggs (separated)
2 oz / 50 g thick honey
1/2 pt / 275 ml milk
1 oz / 25 g gelatine
1 large measure of whisky
1 vanilla pod
1 oz / 25 g caster sugar

For the Base:
slice of Genoese sponge, cut into 3 inch / 7.5 cm discs

To Serve:
4 oz / 110 g toasted oatmeal
1/4 pt / 150 ml crème anglaise
1/4 pt / 150 ml crème anglaise flavoured with Drambuie

Method:

The Bavarois:

1. Whisk the egg yolks until creamy.
2. Boil the milk, honey and whisky and add gradually to the yolks. Return to the heat and stir continuously with a wooden spoon to a coating consistency. Add the gelatine and strain. Allow to cool.
3. Lightly whip the cream and fold into the mixture.
4. Whisk the egg whites and sugar until stiff and fold into the mixture.

The Base:

1. Cut four rounds of Genoese sponge with a 3 inch / 7.5 cm diameter cutter.
2. Place the bases on plates and place a 3 inch / 7.5 cm cutter on each.
3. Fill each cutter with Bavarois mixture and leave to set for a couple of hours in the fridge.

To Serve:
Remove the cutters and cover the tops with oatmeal. Pour the two sauces around the délices and serve.

Lemon Pudding Soufflé

The tang of lemon partners the lightness of the soufflé perfectly

Serves 6

Ingredients:

1oz / 25g unsalted butter
1oz / 25g plain flour
1oz / 25g caster sugar
3 large eggs, separated
½ pt / 150 ml milk
grated zest of one lemon

Method:

1. Heat the milk in a thick-bottomed pan.

2. Soften the butter, then add the flour and sugar.

3. Add the milk, and whisk until smooth. Return to the heat and cook until the mixture comes away from the sides of the pan.

4. Remove from the heat again and beat in the yolks, one at a time.

5. Whisk the whites until stiff. Fold them gently into the mixture.

6. Butter and sugar 6 suitable moulds, such as dariole moulds or ramekins.

7. Fill the moulds about ¾ full and place in a bain-marie. Cook in a hot pre-heated oven, Gas 8 / 450°F / 230°C for 15 to 20 minutes.

8. Turn out onto warm plates, and serve with crème anglaise (see page 121).

Chef's Tip: Put half the sugar in the milk when boiling it, as it helps to prevent burning, especially with larger quantities.

To hear most people talk, you would think soufflés were a species of wild, unpredictable animal, waiting to catch amateur chefs unawares. Apparently they are difficult to handle. They are capricious beasts who will do everything they can to thwart your plans for an enjoyable dinner party.

Above all, unlike tame animals, they will never perform party tricks for you. Specifically, they will never sit up and beg (or rise) in the way that you want them to. Let me say here and now that my knowledge of the beast is very different.

It is all a question of organisation. Once you have mastered this, the soufflé will become one of your standby "easy" dishes, and will earn you the praise and plaudits of your guests into the bargain!

The egg whites can be whipped up in 10 minutes while your guests are savouring the end of their main course. Grease the ramekins well, and make sure the oven is fully heated before putting them in. They will rise perfectly every time!

See also Courgette Soufflé for further tips (see page 15).

February

Al's father had walked out one night to get some firewood in the forest, and had never returned.

One wild winter's evening, his stepmother sent Al off on a similar errand, even though you wouldn't have put your cat out on such a night.

He walked for miles, until he could not see for the blizzards, and could not feel for the biting cold. But he dared not go back without fuel, for fear of his stepmother's anger.

But just when he thought he could go no further, he came upon a strange group of people seated round a bonfire.

Courgette Soufflé

Fluffy and light, with the delicate flavour of courgettes and air!

Serves 6

Ingredients:

    1 lb / 450 g small, firm courgettes
    1 1/2 oz / 40 g unsalted butter
    1 1/2 oz / 40 g flour
    4 fl oz / 110 ml milk
    3 oz / 75 g Parmesan cheese, grated
    2 egg yolks
    4 egg whites
    salt and pepper
    olive oil

Method:

1. Cut a quarter of the courgettes into small dice (about 1/4 inch / 15 mm) and grate the remainder. Sprinkle a little salt over the courgettes and leave to stand for an hour. Rinse off the salt and dry with kitchen paper.

2. Melt the butter in a thick-bottomed pan, add the flour and cook gently for a few minutes. Gradually add the warmed milk, stirring continuously.

3. Add the grated courgettes and combine well until smooth. Cook for about 10 minutes and allow to cool slightly.

4. Add 2/3 of the cheese and then the egg yolks. Mix well.

5. Fry the diced courgettes in a little hot olive oil until crispy and golden. Drain well on kitchen paper.

6. Whisk the egg whites until they form stiff peaks, then fold them gently into the mixture, adding the diced courgettes and seasoning at the same time.

7. Take six ramekins, grease them well and line with the remaining grated cheese. Divide the mixture between them.

8. Place the ramekins on a roasting tray half filled with hot water. Cook in a pre-heated oven at Gas 5 / 375°F / 190°C, . Bake for 20-25 minutes until well risen and golden on top, and serve immediately.

There is one ingredient in cookery that is responsible for some of the greatest wonders of culinary science. It is used in soufflés and meringues, cakes and puddings, breads and mousses. Yet it costs nothing.

It is responsible for the ripening of cheese, the browning of meat and the opening up of the bouquet of wine. All of these processes produce fascinating and complex flavours, yet the ingredient of which I speak has no flavour itself.

I speak, of course, of air. Champagne is another celebrated example of the effect of air. I have never tasted "still" Champagne, but I don't think it would taste very exciting.

Soufflés are a prime example of the use of air in cookery. They are not difficult, as I said in an earlier recipe. But you must treat them with confidence - they can sense when somebody is frightened! Use a very clean china bowl for preparation, and the best oven-proof china you can get for cooking (to improve heat conduction). Butter the dishes well so that the soufflés rise easily.

Smoked Salmon Pancakes with Cream & Chives

A luxurious filling for Shrove Tuesday

Many couples book their wedding receptions here at Friends. I particularly remember one joyous reception, where the couple had decided to tie the knot after 12 years of friendship.

Quite understandably, they were now impatient to get on with it! Having decided to get married after such a long time, they felt entitled to a short engagement. In fact, it was only just long enough to publish the banns.

This meant there was no time to organise a reception. So they had a small family wedding, followed by a big reception about four months later.

At the reception, the time came for the making of speeches. The bride's father tottered to his feet, looking rather dazed.

He apologised for seeming a little distracted, but explained that his daughter had just told him he was going to be a grandfather. Looking round the room and scratching his head, he told the guests that his daughter was the only girl he knew who could have contrived to get pregnant between the wedding and the reception!

Serves 4 (makes 8 pancakes)

Ingredients:

For the Batter:
3 oz / 75 g plain flour
1 egg
1 pt / 570 ml milk
pinch of salt

For the Filling:
6 oz / 175 g sliced smoked salmon
1 tbsp fresh cut chives
juice of ½ a lemon
½ pt / 275 ml double cream
¼ pt / 150 ml plain yoghurt
mill pepper
sprigs of fresh dill to garnis

Method:

1. Sieve the salt and flour into a bowl and make a well in the centre. Whisk together the egg and milk and gradually beat in the liquid. The batter should be the consistency of single cream.

2. Cook the pancakes in a small non-stick frying pan for a few minutes on each side. Make sure the pan is very hot before adding the batter, which should sizzle immediately on contact with the metal surface.

3. Lay the pancakes out on a flat clean surface. Lay smoked salmon evenly over each one and roll up tightly. Trim the ends neatly.

4. Choose a shallow pan into which the pancakes will fit snugly, and bring the cream to the boil in it. Place the pancakes in the pan and heat through for about 5-8 minutes, turning them once.

5. Remove the pancakes onto hot plates and add to the pan the yoghurt, chives, lemon juice and a few twists of pepper according to taste.

6. Heat gently without boiling, adjust the consistency with warm water as necessary and spoon over the pancakes. Garnish with sprigs of fresh dill and serve as a starter.

Poached Chicken Breast with Vegetables & Herbs

A light and healthy dish, with the flavour of fresh herbs

Serves 4

Ingredients:

 4 breasts of chicken, skinned and trimmed
 2 pts / 1.2 l chicken stock
 4 oz / 110 g baby carrots
 4 oz / 110 g baby turnips
 4 oz / 110 g asparagus spears
 4 oz / 110 g baby leeks
 4 oz / 110 g baby onions
 1 sprig fresh thyme
 1 tbsp roughly chopped English parsley
 1 tbsp chives, cut into short lengths
 5 fl oz / 150ml hazelnut oil
 rock salt

Method:

1. Peel and blanch the vegetables in boiling salted water, separately, for 5 minutes leaving them slightly undercooked. Refresh under cold water. Drain and keep to one side.

2. Bring the stock to the boil in a shallow pan. Add a little rock salt, the thyme and the chicken.

3. Reduce the heat and simmer for about 15 minutes, then add the vegetables.

4. Bring the stock back to the boil for about 2 minutes, then remove from the heat.

5. Add the remaining herbs and allow to infuse for 5 minutes.

6. Remove the chicken and vegetables and place on warm plates.

7. Pour a little of the stock over the chicken, and then drizzle the hazelnut oil over the top. Sprinkle a small amount of the rock salt over the top and serve.

Chef's Tip: The oil and the salt may be omitted for health or dietary reasons.

I first met the "Serial Health Club Junkie" at a party. She told me she had just joined a new health club. It had the most fantastic facilities - including a swimming pool. "My other one doesn't have a pool", she said, petulantly.

"Your other one?"

"Yes I still go there, but I hear there's another one opening up shortly which is going to be the place to go. I'll have to join that as well."

I was stunned. I mean, if I ever found the time to join a health club, I would regard it as simple economics only to join one! I asked her how she found time to go to all the different exercise classes.

She looked at me as though I had just offered her a cigarette at an ASH meeting. "One doesn't go to exercise," she explained, as if to a small child, and one of limited intelligence, at that. "One goes to socialise. That's why the pool is such an asset. There's nothing like a light lunch with the girls by the pool!"

Terrine of Seafish with a Hot Chive Sauce

The salt tang of the sea with a light chive sauce

Page 8

Breast of Pigeon Sautéed with Spinach & Lardons

Succulent game on a bed of spinach

Page 9

Grilled Salmon with Roasted Peppers & Watercress Sauce

As healthy as it is colourful

Page 10

Far right

Lemon Pudding Soufflé

Fresh from the oven!

Page 13

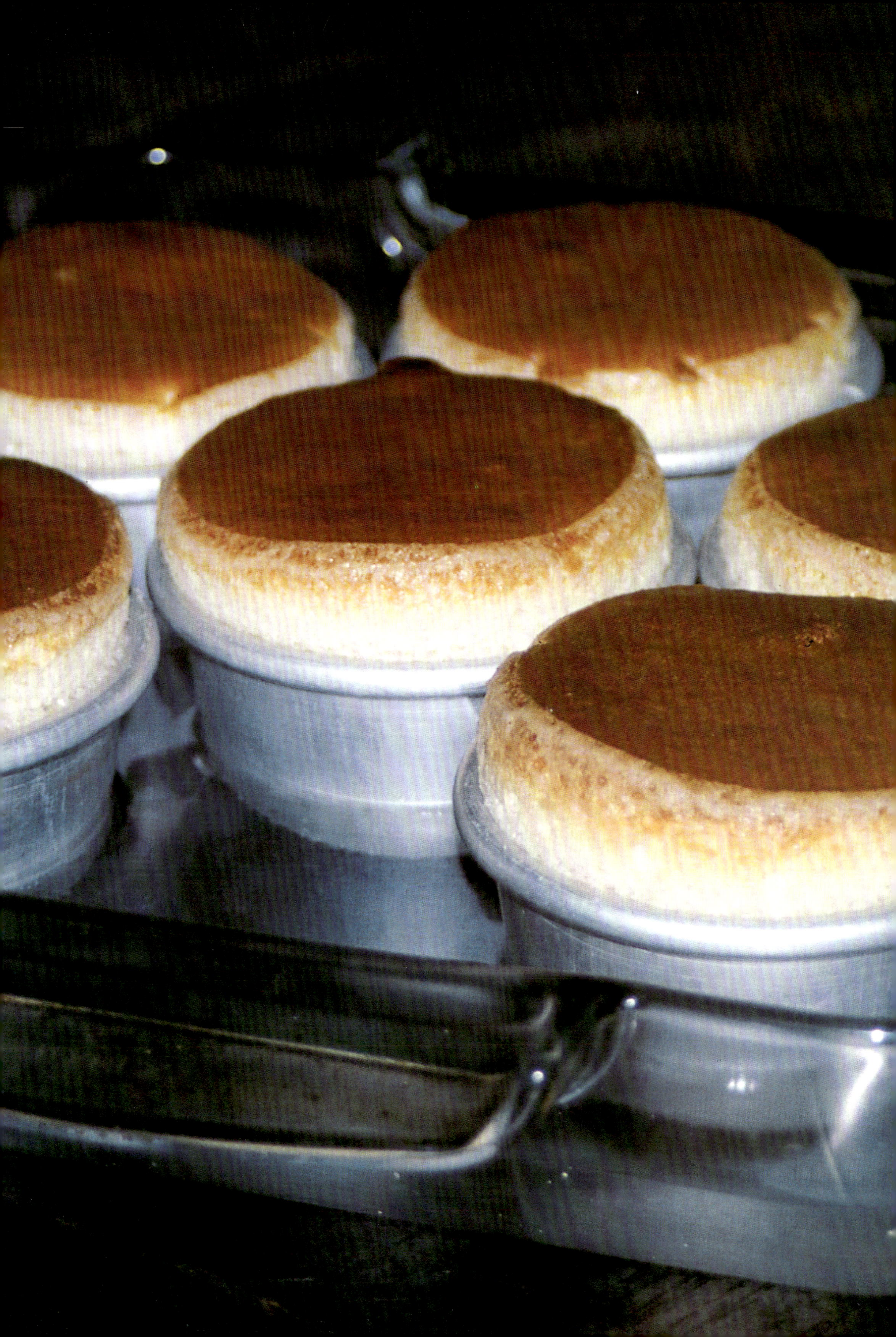

Galette of Aubergines, Tomatoes & Mozzarella

Truly Italian, both in taste and colour

Here is one of two dishes that remind me of the first time my wife and I visited Italy. The second appears later in this book.

We arrived at Pisa airport too late to make the train connection to Florence. On top of this the baggage got temporarily lost and there was a queue at the passport desk. A seasoned Italian traveller standing near to us heaved a heavy sigh. "Jesus Maria", he breathed, "welcome back to Italy."

We fell into conversation with him. I told him about the famous English acronym for his national airline, Alitalia: Aircraft Landing In Tokyo, All Luggage In Athens! He laughed heartily and said we didn't know how true it was!

After standing in the line for about half an hour without moving at all, he turned philosophical:

"A queue is a universal thing. But a queue which goes nowhere is a specially Italian thing."

He shrugged his shoulders and introduced himself as Guido. An appropriate name, for he became our firm friend and guide for the rest of our stay.

Serves 4

Ingredients:

1 lb / 450 g aubergines
3 oz / 75 g onions, finely chopped
1 lb / 450 g plum or beef tomatoes
6 oz / 175 g Buffalo mozzarella
2 cloves garlic, crushed
1 tsp chopped coriander
1 tsp caster sugar
15 fl oz / 425 ml low fat yoghurt
2 tsp cornflour
a little olive oil for frying
salt and black mill pepper

Method:

1. Slice the aubergine thinly. Lay out on a wire rack and sprinkle with salt. Leave to stand for one hour.

2. Pat dry with kitchen paper and fry in olive oil until brown on both sides. Remove from the pan. Allow to drain.

3. Cook the onion and garlic gently in olive oil without colouring.

4. Combine the yoghurt, cornflour, coriander and sugar and add to the onion and garlic. Bring to the boil and season lightly. Remove from the heat.

5. Blanch and peel the tomatoes. Slice the tomatoes and mozzarella into ¼ inch / 5 mm slices.

6. Place 4 large slices of aubergine on a greased baking sheet, leaving a good space between them. Spread a little yoghurt mixture on each slice, followed by tomato, then mozzarella. Continue building up in layers, finishing with a layer of yoghurt.

7. Bake in a hot oven Gas 8 / 450°F / 230°C for 20 minutes until golden brown. Serve immediately on hot plates.

Grape Tart

A sophisticated and visually pleasing dessert

Serves 6-8

Ingredients:

    8 oz / 225 g sweet pastry (see page 124)
    1 1/2 lb / 700 g white grapes (washed, peeled and de-seeded)
    2 oz / 50 g caster sugar
    1 measure Calvados
    2 tsp cornflour
    1/4 pt / 150 ml double cream
    1 egg
    a few drops of lemon juice

Method:

1. Line a 7 inch / 18 mm flan ring with sweet pastry and allow to rest in a cool place for 30 minutes.

2. Line the flan case with foil and a layer of baking beans (as a weight) and bake in a moderate oven for about 30 minutes.

3. Meanwhile, macerate the grapes in a bowl with the sugar and Calvados for about 45 minutes.

4. Whisk together the egg and cream. Add the cornflour and whisk until smooth.

5. Mix in the grapes and their juices, without mashing them. Add a few drops of lemon juice to taste.

6. Pour the filling gently into the pastry case, and bake in a lowish oven Gas 3 / 325°F / 170°C, for about 45 minutes.

7. Allow to cool slightly and serve.

My friend Roger the vicar, is always very untidily dressed. When he arrived in his local parish, he arranged a grand dinner in the church hall, and asked me to prepare it.

He dropped in to see me on his way to the hall. "Are we ready to go then?" he said, rubbing his hands.

"You're not going like that!" I gasped, looking at his jeans and frayed shirt.

"Why not?" he said. "Nobody knows me here yet!"

Recently, to celebrate ten years in the parish, he asked me to plan another grand dinner. On the day, I got a terrible feeling of déjà vu. Sure enough, Roger came in, dressed very similarly to how he had been ten years before. This time, my look said it all.

"Oh come now, Terry. It's all right. Everybody knows me here now!"

Well, I suppose people just don't change. With Roger, what you see is what you get, and that's that. It's true of this dessert as well. Although it presents itself much better than Roger does!

Hot Date & Banana Pudding

One of Friends' all-time favourite desserts

Page 24

Smoked Salmon Pancakes with Cream & Chives

True indulgence for Shrove Tuesday

Page 16

Galette of Aubergines, Tomatoes & Mozzarella

Easy as pizza, but a lot lighter

Page 20

Right

Poached Chicken Breast with Vegetables & Herbs

Simplicity is what Friends' food is all about

Page 17

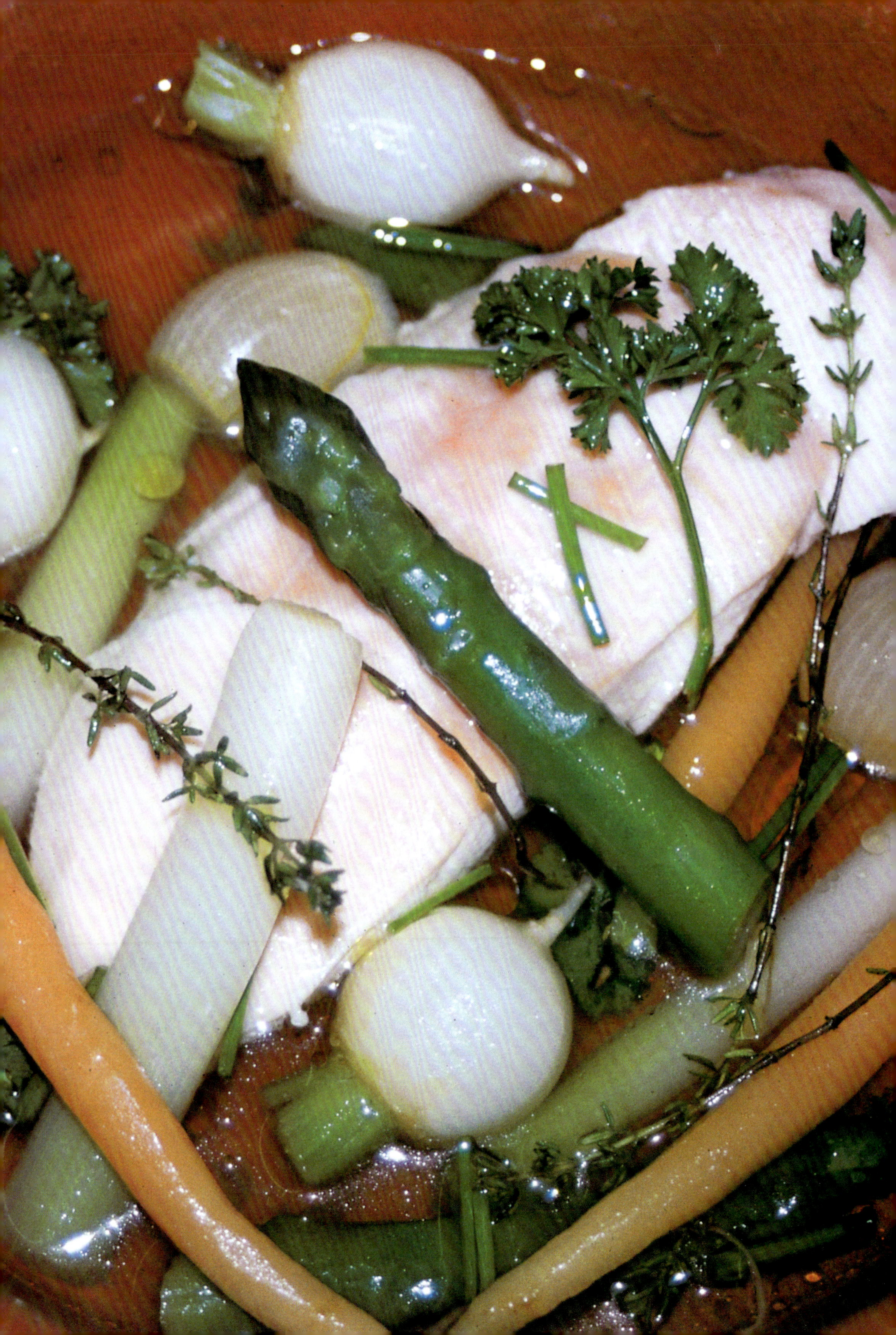

Hot Date & Banana Pudding

A light yet satisfying and warming dessert

Whenever anybody criticises his dress, Roger the Vicar (see previous recipe) likes to tell a story about the well-known Prince of Untidiness, Albert Einstein.

Einstein was repeatedly voted "World's Greatest Man" during his lifetime, and is almost universally accepted as the greatest modern scientist. Yet he certainly owed nothing of this to his dress sense!

Once his wife interrupted a discussion he was having with a friend, to tell him that a US Government official had come to see him. Einstein was in his bare feet, baggy trousers and shirtsleeves.

She suggested that he put on a suit to receive the official. But Einstein, obviously irritated by the unannounced visit and the interruption to his conversation, said:

"Really! If the official wants to see me, here I am. If he wants to see my clothes, show him into the bedroom and open the wardrobe!"

In cookery, appearance is almost as important as substance. So here is one of my favourite desserts, which never fails to please on either count!

Serves 4

Ingredients:

4 oz / 110 g fresh dates (stoneless)
1 level tsp bicarbonate of soda
2 oz / 50 g unsalted butter
3½ oz / 90 g caster sugar
2 medium eggs
4 oz / 110 g plain flour
1 banana

For the Caramel Sauce:

1 cup water
3 oz / 75 g soft brown sugar
3 fl oz / 75 ml double cream

Method:

1. Boil the water and add the dates and bicarbonate of soda. Leave to cool.

2. Cream the butter and sugar and gradually add the beaten eggs. Sift the flour and fold it into the mixture gently.

3. Cut the bananas into ½ inch / 1 cm dice and add to the date mixture.

4. Fold the fruit (including juices) into the creamed butter and flour mix.

5. Pour this sloppy mixture into a greased and lined 6 inch / 15 cm cake tin.

6. Bake in a moderate oven for 50-60 minutes. Test the pudding with the blade of a clean, sharp knife by plunging it into the centre. If it comes out clean, the pudding is cooked through.

7. Towards the end of the cooking time, make the caramel sauce by boiling the water and sugar to form a light caramel. Add the double cream, bring to the boil again and strain.

8. Turn out the pudding and serve with hot caramel sauce.

March

Three of the people got up to welcome Al. One had the face of an old man. But when Al looked at him again, he had the face of a tiny baby. This was January, who looks backwards at the old year and forwards to the new.

Then there was a boy about Al's age, and a young man. January introduced them as February and March.

They showed him wild winds, and frozen streams. And Al looked to see if he could see his father anywhere. But all he saw for miles around was the ravaged landscapes of winter.

*Asparagus &
Smoked Salmon*

Two of the great tastes of early spring

Page 28

*Calves' Liver
with
Bubble & Squeak
& Onion Gravy*

No-nonsense nourishment!

Page 32

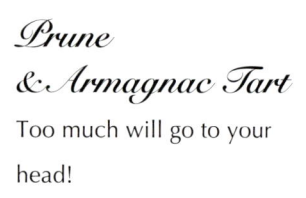

26

*Prune
& Armagnac Tart*

Too much will go to your head!

Page 34

Right

*Fillet of Beef
with Caramelised
Shallots, Wild
Mushrooms
& Red Wine*

A rich confluence of hearty flavours

Page 33

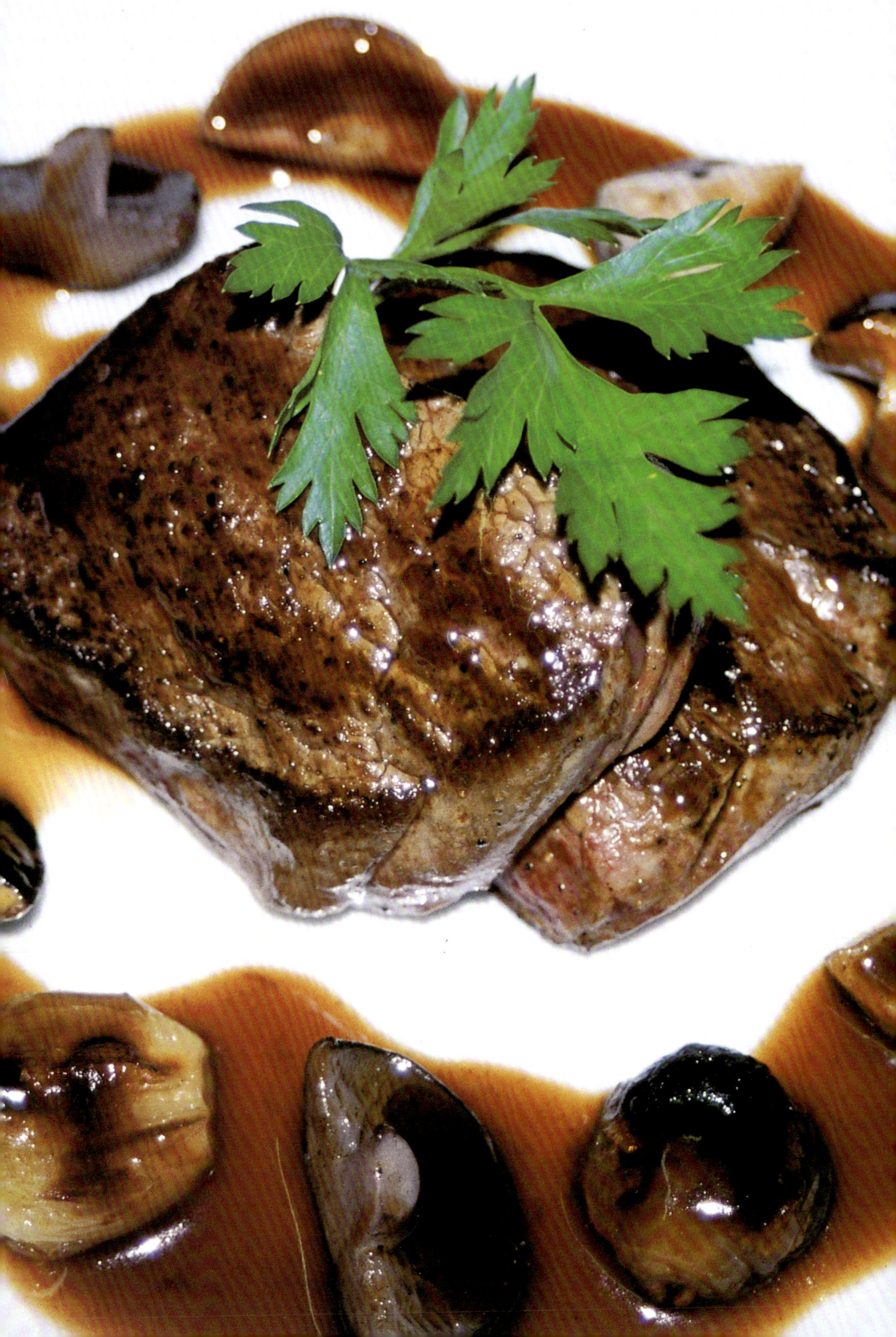

Asparagus wrapped in Smoked Salmon baked in Wafer-Thin Pastry.

A perfect marriage of textures and flavours

This is a story about Sara the Serial Health Club Member. She and her friends join as many health clubs as they can - just to be seen. They never use them for exercise!

I met her at a party, talking to a lady called Samantha. They discovered they were members of some of the same clubs. They were playing one-upmanship, and I listened, fascinated.

Samantha played a high card. She invited Sara to lunch with her at the classiest health club in London. Sara blanched. I knew she wasn't a member there. But she recovered her composure and reached for her pocket diary.

"Darling, it's the most awful bad luck. Tony's taking me to New York for a shopping trip that weekend!"

Then Samantha played her trump card - literally! She produced it with a studied nonchalance (I could tell she was enjoying herself), and handed it to Sara.

"But darling! Why didn't you say! I'm a member at the Metropolitan! It is the place to go in NY at the moment. You simply must borrow my card!

Serves 4

Ingredients:

12 cooked spears of jumbo asparagus, 4 inches / 10 cm in length
4 thin slices smoked salmon (about 2 oz / 50 g each)
4 sheets filo pastry
2 fl oz / 50 ml sunflower oil
6 fl oz / 175 ml natural yoghurt
1 heaped tsp finely cut chives
a few drops of lemon juice
freshly milled black pepper

Method:

1. Lay the filo pastry leaves out flat and brush both sides lightly with the oil. Place a slice of smoked salmon in the centre of each.

2. Lay the asparagus on the salmon and give each portion a twist of the peppermill. Roll up each sheet into a small parcel, Leaving the tips slightly protruding from one end.

3. Place on a lightly greased baking sheet and bake in a moderate oven Gas 6 / 400°F / 200°C for 12-15 minutes until golden brown.

4. Mix the yoghurt with the chives and lemon juice. Adjust to the consistency of double cream by mixing with a little warm water as necessary.

5. Divide the mixture equally onto four warm plates. Place the hot parcels on top and serve immediately.

Salmon Fishcakes

A quick and easy light meal, ideal as a snack or starter

Serves 4

Ingredients:
- 8 oz / 225 g salmon fillet, cooked
- 12 oz / 350 g potatoes
- 1 oz / 25 g unsalted butter
- 2 egg yolks
- 1 tbsp mayonnaise
- 1 tbsp chopped chives
- 4 oz / 110 g fresh breadcrumbs
- salt and mill pepper

Method:

1. Cut the potatoes into even sized pieces and boil them in slightly salted water, until well cooked. Drain well and mash.

2. Flake the fish and add to the potato, together with the melted butter and egg yolks. Add the mayonnaise and chives and season to taste. Leave to cool.

3. Divide the mixture into 8 portions, roll them in the breadcrumbs and shape into cakes. (The idea is to crumb the cakes lightly, so do not use the usual method of "flour, egg and breadcrumbs").

4. Fry the cakes in a little hot vegetable oil, until crisp and golden.

5. Serve with a sauce of your choice. A suggestion would be a hot Tartare sauce, made by adding chopped gherkins, capers and parsley to a little beurre blanc.

We once went to a friend's house for dinner. Not to put too fine a point on it, my wife and I were dreading the experience. Our friend has no interest in food whatsoever, and if you are invited to her house for a meal then it is simply because she thinks it is "her turn".

This time it was worse than ever. She had completely forgotten we were coming. She looked at us in amazement and said "Oh my God! I haven't got a thing in the house! And it's Terry of all people!"

Secretly, my heart was leaping as she said this. Nobody's kitchen is ever completely empty. I found a few dusty potatoes, onions and carrots in the vegetable rack and, lurking at the back, the remains of a cabbage. From these unpromising ingredients I made a passable vegetable soup.

Then, in best Blue Peter style, I went to the boot of the car and brought out the salmon fishcakes I had prepared earlier just in case!

Caramelised Onion & Emmental Tartlet

Ideal for children who won't eat (see story)

Page 38

Confit of Duck with Garlic Mash

A French classic, and a Friends' classic

Page 40

Chocolate Marquise

The vicar's delight!

Page 41

Right

Polenta with Mushrooms & Herbs

Inspired by the Leaning Terry of Pisa (see story)!

Page 39

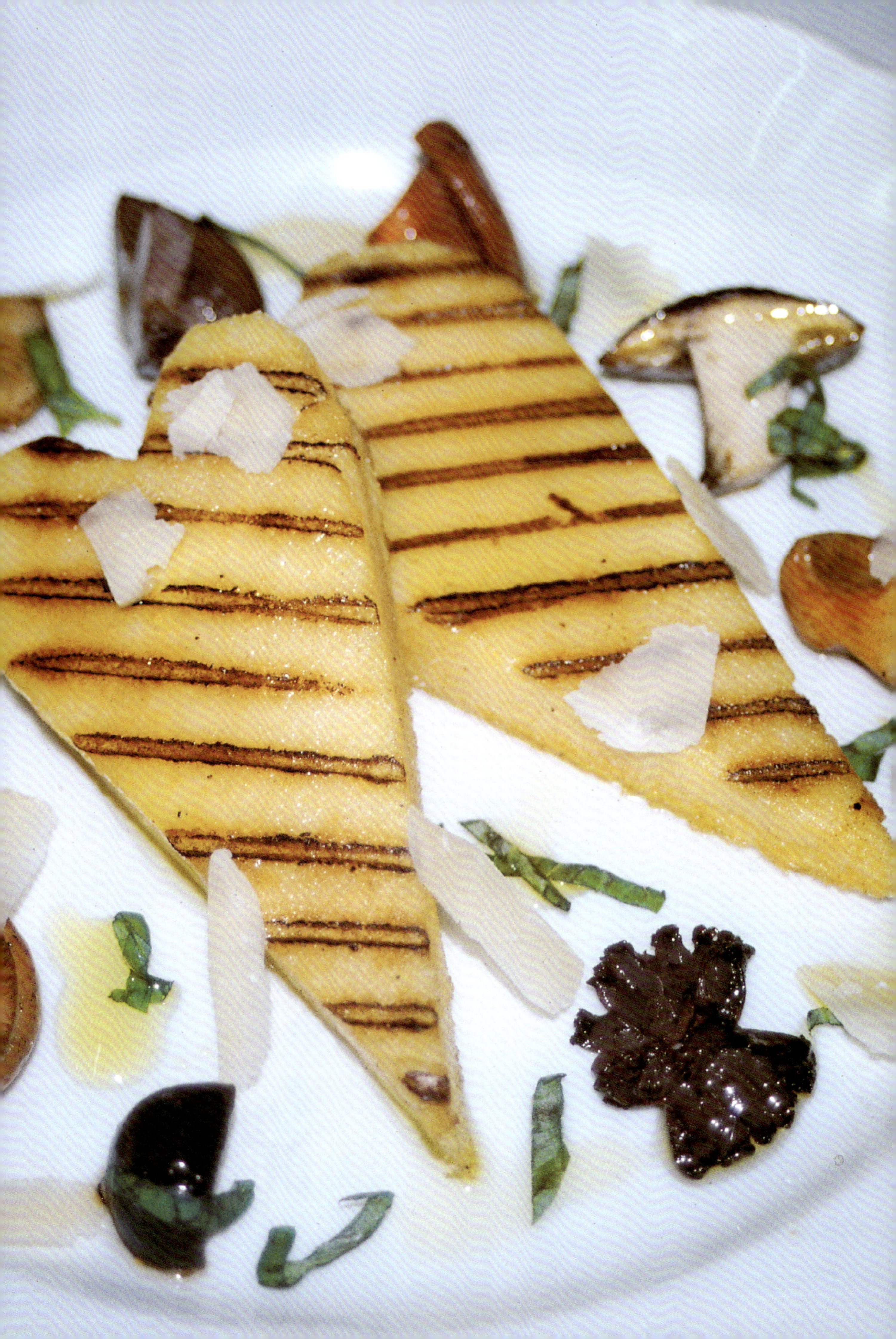

Calves' Liver with Bubble & Squeak & Onion Gravy

Unashamedly simple, nutritious and utterly enjoyable

Another anecdote from the annals of the Farr family's primary philosopher (my son, that is). To spare his blushes I will say that he was much younger when he discovered this secret of eternal youth (if that makes sense!)

He had reached the age where he was passing on from his primary school. He was a little morose at the thought of leaving his friends. I found him sitting on the stairs one day in a trance of introspection, and asked him what the matter was.

"Well, Dad, I've been thinking. I couldn't borrow the washing machine, could I?"

I was very pleased at this sudden interest in domestic chores, and said that of course he could. What did he want it for?

"Well, for myself really. I thought if I went through a wash then I might shrink. Then you'd have to send me back to my old school again!"

Oh would that it were that simple! Alas, it isn't. The best you can do is keep on growing as healthily as possible. Dishes like this one certainly help!

Serves 4

Ingredients:

1 lb / 450 g calves' liver, skinned and thinly sliced
4 oz / 110 g onions, finely sliced
12 oz / 350 g large potatoes (Desirée, if possible)
6 oz / 175 g Savoy cabbage, (washed and finely shredded)
3 oz / 75 g unsalted butter
2 egg yolks
vegetable oil for cooking
1/4 pt / 150 ml red wine sauce (see page 116)
salt, pepper and nutmeg
seasoned flour

Method:

1. Cook the potatoes in boiling salted water until cooked through. Drain well.

2. Melt 2 oz / 50 g butter in a thick-bottomed pan. Add the cabbage, cover with a lid, reduce the heat and cook gently for about 20 minutes.

3. Mash the potatoes in a large bowl. Add the cabbage and egg yolks, seasoning to taste with a little salt, pepper and nutmeg. Shape the mixture into 4 equal cakes and allow to rest in a cool place.

4. Melt the remaining butter in a pan, add the onions and cook for about 20 minutes until they are well coloured or caramelised. Add the red wine sauce, bring to the boil, and check the seasoning and consistency.

5. Heat some oil in a frying pan and coat the liver in seasoned flour. Cook for 2-3 minutes on each side, leaving it slightly pink in the middle.

6. Heat some oil in a clean pan, and fry the bubble and squeak for 2-3 minutes on each side until golden in colour.

7. Place the liver and bubble and squeak on warm plates. Pour a cordon of sauce around the outside and serve.

Fillet of Beef with Caramelised Shallots, Wild Mushrooms & Red Wine

A full-throated dish, rich with deep and complementary flavours

Serves 4

Ingredients:

1 1/2 lb / 700 g beef fillet,
  trimmed and cut into 8 equal slices
4 oz / 110 g unsalted butter
1/2 pt / 275 ml red wine sauce (see page 116)
12 small shallots, peeled
1/4 pt / 150 ml red wine
1 tsp brown sugar
8 oz / 225 g ceps or other suitable mushrooms,
  washed, prepared and quartered
salt and milled pepper
vegetable oil for cooking

Method:

1. Place the shallots in a small pan, with 1 oz / 25 g butter, the sugar, a pinch of salt and the wine. Add enough cold water to cover them completely.

2. Bring to the boil and simmer slowly for about 30 minutes, until the liquid has evaporated and the shallots are cooked and well glazed all over.

3. Season the beef with a little salt and pepper.

4. Heat a little oil and 1 oz / 25 g butter in a pan, and cook the fillets quickly at a high temperature for about 3 minutes on each side. Remove the fillets from the pan and keep warm. At this stage the beef should be medium rare.

5. Add the remaining butter to the same pan and heat until almost brown.

6. Add the mushrooms and cook at a high temperature, seasoning them at the same time. 3 to 4 minutes should be long enough.

7. Place the fillets on warm plates and pour a cordon of hot red wine sauce around each one. Garnish with the shallots and mushrooms and serve.

Chef's Tip: At this time of the year it may not be possible to get fresh wild mushrooms, in which case I recommend that you use dried mushrooms. They are available from most good delicatessens and are far superior to tinned or preserved. (They tend to have a more intense flavour than even the fresh fungus).

When one of my sons was about five, he had a special friend in his first year at school. They were inseparable, and visited each other's houses almost every week. But when they went back to school after the summer holidays, Robert was hardly mentioned again.

I asked my son what had happened to Robert, and why he never talked about him any more.

"Oh", he said philosophically, "he's a fading-away friend".

How sad, but how true. Throughout our lives our friends fade away, and new ones arrive on the scene. But I couldn't help seeing another image in my mind - that of poor Robert literally wasting away through lack of nourishment! (It was probably something to do with the fact that I work with food all the time!)

So in honour of the fading-away friend, I composed a tasty, nourishing dish with prime beef fillet at its centre. And if Robert is reading this, he's welcome to come and restore himself to health any time!

Prune & Armagnac Tart

A full-flavoured dessert, heady and hedonistic

Serves 8

Ingredients:
- 6 oz / 175 g dried stoneless prunes
- 1/8 pt / 75 ml Armagnac
- 8 oz / 225 g frangipane (see page 123)
- 6 oz / 175 g apricot jam
- 1 lb / 450 g sweet pastry (see page 124)

Method:

1. Soak the prunes in the Armagnac overnight, during which time the liquid will be completely absorbed.

2. Roll out the pastry and use it to line a lightly greased 8 inch / 20 cm flan ring. Leave to rest in the refrigerator for 30 minutes.

3. Line the flan case with foil and a layer of baking beans, and bake blind in a moderate oven, Gas Mark 7 / 425°F / 220°C for about 25 minutes. Remove the foil and beans, and return to the oven for another 10 minutes.

4. Spread half the jam over the base of the flan, then place the prunes evenly over the jam.

5. Spread the frangipane over the prunes, and bake in a moderately low oven, Gas 4 / 350°F / 180°C for 1 1/4 hours.

6. Warm the remaining jam and glaze the top of the flan with a soft pastry brush. Serve warm.

Chef's Tip: You can now buy some very good dried prunes, which don't need to be soaked for so long. Especially useful if you have to make the flan at short notice!

When I was a boy I used to love the Nutcracker Suite. My Grandpa Hugo introduced me to it, but he was never one to leave a story alone. He would always try to develop the plot in new and unpredictable directions. I think it was from him that I inherited some of the ability to think creatively, both in cookery and in writing about it!

One day, he told me what happened to the Sugar Plum Fairy in later life.

Apparently she took to visiting the Mediterranean resorts, where she was much admired as a belle of the beach. Unfortunately, she became addicted to the high life, and did too much sunbathing. Eventually she dried out completely, and became a Sugar Prune Fairy.

Much embittered, she developed a taste for strong liquor. She became a connoisseur of Armagnac, and that was to be her undoing. For one day she lay down upon a pastry base in a drunken heap, and never woke up.

That, according to the wisdom of Grandpa Hugo, is the origin of this dish!

Chocolate Soufflé

This is a simple version that I make at home for my family

Serves 4-6

Ingredients:
- 1/2 pt / 275 ml milk
- 4 oz / 110 g plain chocolate
- 3 oz / 75 g caster sugar
- 3 egg yolks
- 5 egg whites
- 1 oz / 25 g cornflour
- a pinch of salt
- icing sugar to finish

Method:

1. Dilute the cornflour with a little of the milk, put the remainder of the milk in a thick-bottomed pan and bring to the boil. Add the chocolate and 2 oz / 50 g of the sugar, and stir until completely melted.

2. Add the cornflour paste gradually, stirring continuously, then remove from the heat.

3. Beat in the yolks one at a time, until completely combined.

4. Prepare a 2 pt / 1.2 l soufflé dish by greasing it well and sugaring the inside.

5. Whisk the whites with a pinch of salt until they form soft peaks, then add the remaining sugar and whisk until firm peaks form.

6. Mix in a quarter of the whites until well blended, then fold in the remainder carefully.

7. Pour the mixture into the dish, and bake in the centre of the oven, Gas 5 / 375°F / 190°C for about 45 minutes. dust with the icing sugar and serve immediately.

Chef's Tip: The basic preparation can be done in advance, up to step 4. If this is the case, warm the mixture slightly when continuing from step 5 onwards.

Once Easter has been and gone, I always know one local vicar will be very pleased about it - my friend Roger. "Thank goodness that's over!" he said to me one year.

I was shocked. I mean, Easter is what Christianity is all about, isn't it? For the professionals, I mean. The rest of us get all excited about Christmas, forgetting that, in religious terms, it slightly misses the point. But the vicars - they ought to know better!

When I quizzed him on this, he looked a little embarrassed. It wasn't the Easter celebrations he was glad to be finished with. They were a joyous occasion for him, if very hard work.

No, his sigh of relief was caused by a simple addiction. One which, as a chef, I know afflicts a large section of the population. Vicars are only human, after all. And Roger suffers from a deep craving for chocolate. Particularly very fine, dark chocolate. The only difference from the rest of us is that he takes giving it up for Lent very seriously indeed!

April

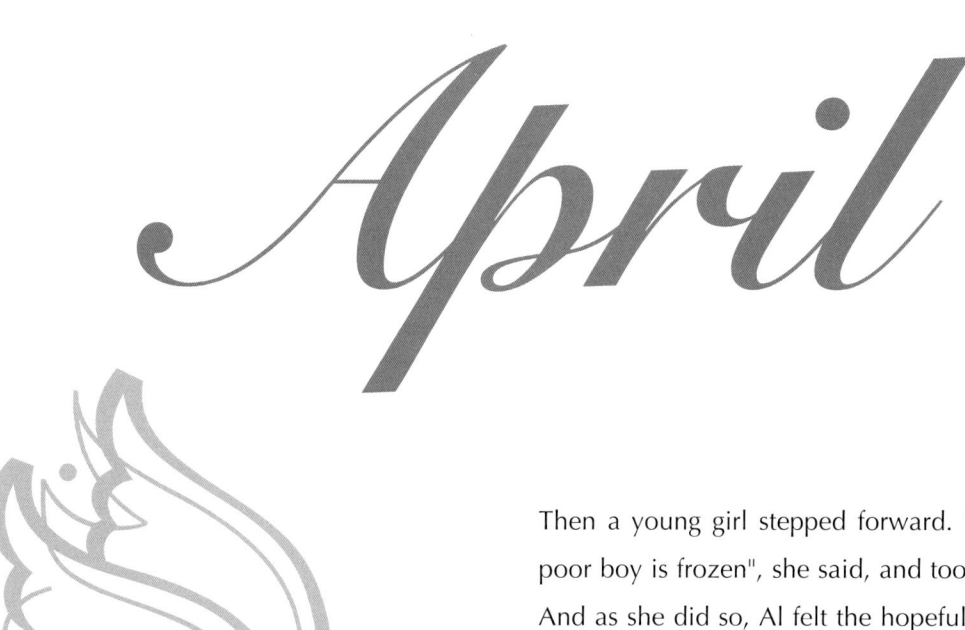

Then a young girl stepped forward. "Come, the poor boy is frozen", she said, and took his hand. And as she did so, Al felt the hopeful warmth of spring spread throughout his body.

This was April, and her beautiful pale face was framed with garlands of blue and white.

She led him through banks of bluebells and violets, singing as she went. The tune was mournful, but with merry snatches that came and went like showers of gentle rain. And as they walked together, it seemed that her song thawed the streams and wakened the slumbering earth.

Marinated Salmon

This recipe has been consistently popular at Friends, and must be attributed to Ben!

Serves 6

Ingredients:

18 oz / 500 g Salmon Fillet, skinned, trimmed of any
fat and blood, but above all, very fresh!
1 tbsp of chopped dill
4 juniper berries
¼ pt / 50ml
⅛ pt white wine vinegar
1 dssp of Dijon mustard
1 dssp of caster sugar
6 black peppercorns, finely crushed
juice of half a lemon
pinch of sea salt

Method:

1. Blend all the ingredients, apart from the salmon, in a food processor until very smooth

2. Slice the salmon at an angle, into fine slices, lay them on a plastic or stainless steel tray.

3. Spread the marinade over the salmon, cover with cling film, and refrigerate for 24 hours.

4. To serve, trickle a little sour cream over the salmon, and garnish with a little tossed salad.

    Chef's Tip: Don't be put off by thinking this is raw salmon, the marination process effectively cooks the fish.

Salmon is one of the most versatile of fish. It has a distinctive delicate flavour that can be enhanced to a greater or lesser degree according to the method of preparation.

In the Middle Ages it was one of the most popular of fish. But popularity often leads to scarcity. Certainly if the current levels of overfishing continue then we may look forward to all our common fish, such as cod and haddock, attaining the luxury status that salmon has recently enjoyed.

And conversely, the widespread techniques of salmon farming may well result in salmon's losing that luxury status before long for all but those who insist on eating the wild variety.

Salmon responds well to most methods of cooking. It can be lightly poached, or seared on a hot skillet with chilli. It can be eaten cold or hot, raw or cooked, in rillettes (see rillettes of duck post) or in sandwiches, smoked or marinated. Here is a simple recipe for marinated salmon.

Caramelised Onion & Emmental Tartlet

A variation on the classic combination of the flavours of cheese and onion

I found this recipe in the heart of Alsace, in the town of Rouffach, and adapted it to my own style. Traditionally it is a food for children going through a "non-eating" phase.

Apparently the original tart was baked by an exasperated mother whose son refused to eat. Eventually she said "Right, if you want to eat nothing, then I'll cook you something out of nothing!"

She took her best Emmental cheese from just across the border and showed him the huge holes. Then she sliced up her tastiest onions from the garden into rings and showed him their empty centres.

The son was unconvinced, and they continued arguing for so long that the onions cooked to the stage of caramelisation. But when the son tasted it he was immediately won over and said: "Mummy, I never knew nothing tasted so good!"

And in a typically French happy ending, he grew up to be a famous chef. I don't know about the truth of the story, but I hope you'll agree that nothing can sometimes taste absolutely fantastic!

Serves 4

Ingredients:

For the Tartlet Bases:
8 oz / 225 g shortcrust pastry (see page 125)

For the Filling:
2 oz / 50 g cold unsalted butter
1 lb / 450 g Spanish onions, sliced
6 oz / 175 g Emmental cheese, grated

For the Custard:
3 egg yolks
2 pts / 1.2 l semi-skimmed milk
salt, freshly ground black pepper and freshly grated nutmeg

To Serve and Garnish:
fresh salad leaves
beetroot pieces
a little sour cream

Method:

1. Roll out the pastry on a lightly-floured surface and use it to line the tartlet moulds. Leave to rest for 1 hour in the fridge.

2. Melt the butter in a thick-bottomed pan, add the onions and cook gently for about 30 minutes, until the onions are caramelised.

3. Prick the tartlet cases and line them with silver foil. Weight them with baking beans or a variety of dried beans. Bake blind in a preheated moderate oven Gas 5 / 375°F / 190°C for 20 minutes. Remove the foil and divide the caramelised onions equally among the tartlet cases.

4. Make the custard by whisking together the egg yolks and the semi-skimmed milk. Season with salt, pepper and grated nutmeg to taste.

5. Add the custard to the filled tartlets and top with the grated cheese. Return to the oven and bake for 35 minutes.

6. Turn out the finished tartlets and serve on a bed of salad leaves. Garnish with a little beetroot and soured cream.

Polenta with Mushrooms & Herbs

Simple herbs and seasoning bring out the flavour of mushrooms perfectly

Serves 4

Ingredients:

- 8 oz / 225 g polenta
- 2 pts / 1.2 l water
- 6 oz / 175 g mushrooms, preferably chanterelles or ceps, but any mushrooms of your choice will do
- 2 tbsp basil, roughly shredded
- 2 tbsp olive oil

Method:

1. Boil the water and beat the polenta into it gradually with a wooden spoon until it is smooth and well mixed.

2. Return to the heat and cook gently for about 45 minutes, stirring constantly and making sure the mixture does not burn.

3. The polenta is cooked when it readily comes away from the sides of the pan. Turn out into a lightly greased roasting tray or baking sheet and spread evenly to a thickness of about 1/2 inch / 1 cm. Allow to cool and set firmly.

4. When the mixture is set, cut into diamond shapes about 2 inches / 5 cm long, or any other shapes which you prefer.

5. Lightly brush the pieces with olive oil and place on a hot chargrill or under a hot grill until crispy and golden.

6. Meanwhile, heat a little olive oil in a shallow pan. Cook the mushrooms quickly and season with a little salt and milled pepper. Mix in the basil.

7. Place the polenta in a hot serving dish and add the mushrooms and herbs. Garnish with Parmesan shavings and serve.

In an earlier recipe I told how my wife and I once made a made a friend at Pisa airport. He showed us to a little trattoria and recommended the following dish, praising the mushrooms as "mirabile".

I was tired after the airport and I also had one too many glasses of the excellent Chianti. In fact, I was totally Pisa'ed! I cannot remember much more, but my wife assures me that we stepped out into the Festival of Lights, which was in full swing at the time. Apparently when I saw the lights I thought I was hallucinating. I even accused our new friend Guido of feeding us "magic" mushrooms, having misunderstood the word "mirabile"!

Guido showed us to a hotel, and we all went to our room for a night-cap. But according to legend, I simply went and stood beside the bed, tottered for a moment, then keeled over and fell asleep.

We remain friends with Guido to this day. And he very much enjoys telling the tale of when he met the "Leaning Terry of Pisa"!

Confit of Duck with Garlic Mash

One of our favourite dishes at Friends

This recipe is one of Friends Restaurant's specialities. So I thought I would give a little account of the origins of this historic dish.

It started, like many other ancient dishes that have survived to the present day, as a method of preserving food. In modern times we enjoy the luxury of exercising our culinary skills mainly in the service of gastronomic enjoyment. But in ancient times a recipe often had to have a functional aspect as well.

It is highly prized in the Gers, Périgord and Landes regions because of its longevity and delicate flavour. It is sometimes used as an ingredient in the preparation of other dishes, but is more often enjoyed in its own right as a meat dish with various accompaniments, depending on regional specialities.

At Friends we favour duck confit, but goose, turkey and pork confit are also popular. Chicken, rabbit, guinea fowl, woodcock and veal confit can also be found littering the menus of southwestern France. At Friends we serve it with a simple garlic mash.

Serves 4

Ingredients:

For the Confit:
4 large duck legs,
   preferably Barbary or Gressingham
4 bay leaves, cut into pieces
1 small bunch fresh thyme
2 tbsp rock salt
4 cloves garlic, peeled and thinly sliced
sufficient vegetable oil (or preferably duck fat)
   to cover the duck while cooking

For the Mash:
2 lb / 900 g King Edwards
   or other suitable mashing potatoes
2 cloves garlic, peeled and finely chopped or puréed
1/4 pt / 150 ml double cream
salt, pepper and olive oil to taste

Method:

The Confit:

1 Lay the trimmed duck legs on a tray and sprinkle evenly with the rock salt, herbs and garlic.

2 Leave the duck to "dry marinade" in a cool place for a few hours.

3 Remove all the herbs and spices. Place the cleaned legs in a pot and cover with the fat or oil.

4 Bring to the boil, cover with a lid or foil, and place in a moderate oven Gas 6 / 400°F / 200°C for about 90 minutes. The duck is cooked when a sharp knife can be inserted and removed easily.

5 Drain the duck and place on a baking sheet. Brown under a hot grill or in a very hot oven until brown and crisp.

The Mash:

1 Boil the peeled and quartered potatoes in salted water until well cooked. Drain and mash until smooth.

2 Warm the cream in a pan and add the potatoes with the garlic and a little olive oil. Mix well, heat through and season to taste.

3 To serve, spoon a portion of mash into the middle of a warm plate and place a duck leg on top. Surround with a sauce or gravy of your choice, preferably red wine sauce (see page 116).

Chocolate Marquise

A truly sinful dish that must never be eaten until after Lent!

Serves 8

Ingredients:
- 12 oz / 350 g plain dark chocolate
- 5 1/2 oz / 160 g unsalted butter
- 3 1/2 oz / 100 g caster sugar
- 4 eggs, separated
- 1 measure crème de menthe

Method:

1. Whisk the egg yolks and half the sugar together in a large bowl and add 1/2 cup of water. Place the bowl over a pot of simmering hot water and whisk to a creamy consistency. Be careful not to cook for too long or you will have to make some toast to serve them up as scrambled eggs! Ideally it should take about 5 minutes.

2. Break the chocolate into small pieces and add to the yolks. Whisk until smooth and completely melted. Add the crème de menthe and leave to cool.

3. Whisk the egg whites vigorously until they form firm peaks. Add the remaining sugar and whisk until stiff peaks form. Fold (do not whisk) into the cooled chocolate, adding a few drops of hot water if necessary to aid the process.

4. Line a mould or terrine with clingfilm and spoon the mixture in, tapping the base gently to ensure that no air is trapped in the mixture. Leave to set overnight.

5. Turn out when required and cut carefully with a hot knife. Serve with crème anglaise flavoured with a little crème de menthe, or a raspberry coulis with clotted cream.

Every Easter heralds the reunion of Roger the vicar with the greatest love of his life - after his family and the Church that is - chocolate!

Every year his wife buys him an enormous dark chocolate egg, which sits winking seductively at him all through Lent. One Easter we decided to play a little joke on him.

Roger tore his way through the Easter morning service and raced straight over to the vicarage. He burst into the house and reached for his egg. But it was gone!

Frantically, he scrabbled through the cupboards.

"What are you looking for, Roger?" asked his wife, all innocence.

"My egg! Where's my egg?" he pleaded, eyes rolling wildly.

"Oh, that. Terry came by and asked if he could use it for one of his recipes. The local shops had run out of chocolate, apparently."

From the kitchen, I could imagine his face. I hadn't the heart to prolong his agony. I stepped out and presented him with his egg - reincarnated as this Chocolate Marquise. I now make it specially for him every Easter!

Pear and Almond Tart

The simple fan effect gives a professional edge to this delicate tart

We have a regular customer who has "stars in her eyes". We then had a chef called Bob Sinatra, and I suggested she try the pear and almond tart, as it was Mr Sinatra's favourite.

"M - Mr Sinatra?"

"That's right. Our chef. Bob Sinatra".

She looked crestfallen. But then she said: "But he is related to...you know who, is he?" "Oh, yes", I replied. "He's his nephew."

Afterwards she told Bob how much she admired his uncle's work. He looked surprised, then said: "Yes, I suppose he is quite good at it."

"Quite good? He was a pioneer. He paved the way for so many people."

"Oh, I see what you mean. But he did my garden path recently and one of the stones is loose. I'll have to get him round to fix it."

She looked at me witheringly. "Well, I do know who he's related to", I said, "Ronnie Sinatra, the landscape gardener who did my patio!"

Serves 8

Ingredients:

4 large pears "I prefer Comice for this recipe"
1 pt / 570 ml water
4 oz / 110 g granulated sugar
1 vanilla pod (split)
8 oz / 225 g frangipane, (see page 123)
6 oz / 175 g apricot jam
1 lb / 450 g sweet pastry, (see page 124)

Method:

1. Peel the pears, cut them in half and scoop out the pips and core.

2. Make a syrup by simmering the water, sugar and vanilla pod for 20 minutes.

3. Poach the pears in the syrup for about 20 minutes, until just cooked. Allow to cool in the syrup.

4. Roll out the pastry and use it to line a lightly greased 8 inch / 20 cm flan ring. Allow to rest in the fridge for 30 minutes.

5. Line the flan case with foil and a layer of baking beans, and bake blind in a moderately hot oven, Gas 7 / 425°F / 220°C for about 25 minutes. Remove the foil and beans, and return to the oven for another 10 minutes.

6. Spread half the jam over the base of the flan case.

7. Drain the pears, place them cut side down on a board, and cut them into fans, by slicing them from the base of the pear almost to the top.

8. Place the pear fans evenly around the flan. Spread the frangipane over the top.

9. Bake in a moderately low oven, Gas 4 / 350°F / 180°C for about $1^{1/4}$ hours.

10. Warm the remaining jam and glaze the flan, using a soft pastry brush. Serve warm with a little crème anglaise.

May

"This is my sister, May", said April, introducing a tall, willowy girl, whose complexion glowed like the blossoms that were now thronging the branches of the trees. "She will help you find what you want."

"Please, May, I'm looking for firewood to take back for my stepmother", said Al.

May looked very grave. "Is that all you want?" she asked.

"No", said Al thoughtfully. "What I really want is my father. But he is long gone. I do not expect that you can help me find him."

"You may be right", said May, "but we shall see. Now come and meet my sisters."

Duck Livers with Balsamic Vinegar & Almonds

A starter of great character with the musky tang of balsamic vinegar

Serves 4

Ingredients:

1 lb / 450 g duck livers, trimmed of any fat and gristle
1/4 pt / 150 ml balsamic vinegar
4 oz / 110 g toasted, flaked almonds
3 oz / 75 g raisins
vegetable oil for cooking
salt and milled pepper

Method:

1. Heat some oil in a frying pan, and cook the lightly seasoned livers quickly at a high temperature for about 5 minutes, leaving them slightly pink in the middle. Remove from the pan and keep warm.

2. Add the vinegar to the pan and bring to the boil. Add the raisins and heat them through, allowing them to absorb some of the vinegar.

3. Place a little tossed salad in the centre of the plates and place the livers on top. Pour the juices and raisins over the livers and sprinkle with almonds. Serve immediately.

Chef's Tip: Do not overcook the livers or they will become hard and bitter.

One day I bumped into my friend Champagne Charlie. I was overjoyed to see him, and invited him for lunch the next day. I knew just what I would prepare for the starter - fresh oysters. When I had known him years before he had eaten them at every opportunity, preferably with a bottle of Champagne.

But when I served them up the next day, he apologised. "Sorry, Terry. I never touch those now. Had a bad experience with one once, you know." I started on about their being perfectly safe if you made sure they were fresh, but he cut me short.

"I know, Terry. But this experience had nothing to do with digestion".

Apparently he had once gone to a restaurant with a girlfriend. He had ordered his traditional starter, and was happily tucking in when something very strange happened...

As he refused to touch the oysters, I made this starter for him. And if you want to hear the end of the story, go to the recipe for Halibut in Vermouth with Black Noodles on page 85.

Bulwinkle's Mackerel Brandade

A classic dish originating in the Languedoc and Provence regions of France

Serves 4

Ingredients:
- 2 lb / 900 g mackerel, skinned and filleted
- 2 cloves garlic, chopped
- 4 oz / 110 g cream cheese
- 2 tbsp olive oil
- lemon juice, salt and mill pepper to taste

Method:

1. Poach the fish in a little water with the olive oil, garlic and a little seasoning. Allow to cool.

2. Blend the fish and the cooking juices until smooth.

3. Add the cream cheese and blend with the fish until homogeneous. Season to taste and serve as a starter, with crisp salad and croutons, or as a snack with crusty French bread.

N.B: This is not the classical Brandade which uses dried salted fish and potato to absorb the strong flavours.

My son and I once took a south coast fishing trip with a real old salt called Captain Bulwinkle (believe it or not!). We shared the boat with some other very experienced fishermen, one of whom caught a very fine gurnard. He started wondering aloud what on earth he could do with the beast.

"Stuff it!" I said.

"What a brilliant idea!", he replied. Can you help?"

"Certainly", I said. "I'm a taxidermist!"

I explained how I had stuffed all manner of animals: chickens, turkeys, pigs, sheep, cattle, ostrich, haddock, cod, trout, salmon. The list goes on and on, I told him. "So you must have quite a large collection", he asked.

"Actually, no", I replied. "I find that people come along and eat them almost as soon as I've stuffed them!"

He looked horrified, until I explained to him the context of the particular kind of stuffing I do. In the end I left him with this recipe for mackerel brandade, in case I had put him off the idea of eating stuffed fish!

Guinea Fowl with Yellow Pepper Coulis

A felicitous marriage of colours gives a foretaste of a perfect marriage of flavours

Here is a recipe conceived whilst on holiday in Normandy some years ago. Those of you who know me will be aware that my tourism normally takes the form of touring the food markets of wherever I happen to be. They are a great source of inspiration.

It was a warm spring morning, and I was standing gazing at the array of poultry in its abundant variety. I was looking for ideas for what to cook for dinner for my family and friends. My eyes were particularly drawn to some succulent-looking corn-fed guinea fowl at the back of the stall.

As I raised my eyes to ask a question of the stallholder, my eyes came to rest on a magnificent backdrop of brilliant yellow capsicums. They shone in my eyes like the golden apples of the Hesperides, and a marriage was instantly made in my mind with the corn-rich flesh of the guinea fowl. They were obviously made for each other! This recipe was the result.

Serves 4

Ingredients:

2 x cleaned guinea fowl, about $2^{3/4}$ lb / 1.25 kg each
2 oz / 50 g minced chicken,
 blended with an egg white and 1 tbsp of double cream
1 oz / 25 g pink peppercorns
1 oz / 25 g unsalted butter
3 oz / 75 g chopped shallots
8 oz / 225 g yellow peppers (capsicums), diced
$1/4$ pt / 150 ml dry white wine
$1/4$ pt / 150 ml double cream
4 oz / 110 g red, green and yellow peppers,
 cut into julienne (thin strips)
salt and mill pepper

Method:

1. Remove the suprêmes (breasts) and legs from the carcasses and season. Bone the legs and flatten slightly with a cutlet bat or flat of a cleaver.

2. Season the insides of the legs and spread with the chicken combined with the peppercorns.

3. Melt the butter in a thick-bottomed pan, and add the supremes and legs. Cover with a lid.

4. Cook gently for 8-10 minutes. Remove the suprêmes and cook the legs for a further 5-6 minutes. Keep the joints in a warm place in a covered dish.

5. Add the shallots to the pan juices and cook without colouring. Add the diced yellow peppers and cook gently for about 5 minutes. Add the white wine and cook to reduce by half.

6. Add the cream and cook gently for a further 5 minutes.

7. Liquidise the sauce and strain through a fine sieve. Adjust the consistency, with a little stock or warm water, and season to taste.

8. Arrange the suprêmes on one side of the warmed plates and the leg, cut into 5 slices, on the other.

9. Surround the joints with the sauce and garnish the centre with the julienne of mixed peppers and serve.

Salmon Baked in Filo Pastry

Tender tasty salmon enfolded in crispy flaky pastry make this a certainty

Serves 4

Ingredients:

    4 x 5 oz / 150 g salmon fillets
    2 oz / 50 g salmon trimmings
    1 egg white
    1 tbsp chopped tarragon
    1 tsp pink peppercorns
    2 tbsp double cream
    4 sheets filo pastry
    2 oz / 50 g melted unsalted butter
    salt and mill pepper
    ½ pt / 275 ml beurre blanc (see page 115)
    1 tbsp shredded basil
    3 large tomatoes, skinned, deseeded and diced

Method:

1. Make a mousse by blending the salmon trimmings and egg white in a food processor. Add the cream, tarragon and peppercorns and season to taste.
2. Make an incision in the salmon pieces and pipe in the mousse.
3. Butter the sheets of filo and wrap the stuffed salmon in them.
4. Bake in a hot oven for 15-20 minutes until golden brown.
5. Make the sauce by heating the beurre blanc, then add the basil and tomatoes and season to taste.
6. Pour the sauce onto hot plates and present the salmon on top. Serve with new potatoes and crisp green vegetables.

My friend Champagne Charlie once told me a story from his misspent youth, when he was forced to try to make a living from his talents at the snooker tables.

Now Charlie can play a bit. But that day he lost. He offered to play "Double or Quits" for the cool £5,000 riding on the match, but his opponent would have none of it. So Charlie offered an extra incentive. He would play his opponent left-handed if he would give him the chance to win the money back. At last the opponent agreed.

What Charlie hadn't told him was that he is naturally left-handed, but that he had taught himself to play almost as well right-handed. (He thought it might be useful one day!) Now the opponent was asking for "Double or Quits".

They played again and Charlie duly won, ending the day up by £10,000. "The lesson is", Charlie told me, "only bet on certainties!" So here is a sure-fire certainty of a recipe for your next dinner party. (It tastes best if you cook it left-handed!)

Orange Bread & Butter Pudding

An old school dinners favourite with a modern twist

Serves 4-6

Ingredients:

1 pt / 570 ml milk
2 eggs
4 oz / 110 g caster sugar
a few drops of vanilla essence
grated zest of 1 orange
1 small baguette (1 day old)
2 oz / 50 g sultanas
3 oz / 75 g unsalted butter
2 tbsp apricot jam
1 tbsp water

Method:

1. Wash the sultanas and sprinkle into a slightly greased ovenproof dish.
2. Slice the baguette and butter each slice. Arrange over the sultanas.
3. Mix the eggs, sugar, vanilla essence and orange zest in a bowl. Boil the milk, add it to the mixture and mix well.
4. Pour the mixture over the bread and sultanas, allowing the mixture to soak into the bread for a few minutes.
5. Cook in a bain-Marie in a preheated oven Gas 5 / 375°F / 190°C for 35 minutes.
6. Remove from the oven when cooked and allow to cool for a few minutes. Heat the apricot jam and water in a pan and brush this glaze lightly over the surface of the pudding.

Chef's Tip: When boiling the milk add half the amount of sugar to the milk. This will stop the milk from burning.

Bread and butter pudding is one of those great British favourites. It sits there on the table with fish and chips and roast beef and Yorkshire pudding as a prime example of these islands' love of simple yet nourishing and satisfying food.

When I was at school, it was one of the cornerstones of the dessert (sorry, pudding) repertoire, along with spotted dick, roly poly pudding and semolina. From what I understand of modern school menus, you are more likely to get something on the model of a fast food outlet than a "proper" meal, which I (and, I believe, many other chefs) find extremely sad.

But I do seem to remember that I had to be educated into enjoying school food. For the first few weeks I found it repulsive. But thereafter I ate it indiscriminately, and in quantities as large as I could get. Certainly I didn't like my first taste of bread and butter pudding. But soon I couldn't get enough of it, and that continues to this day. Here is Friends' slightly altered version.

Apple & Calvados Tart

My reconstruction of the now infamous "Bar Rio" dessert

Serves 8

Ingredients:

- 1 lb / 450 g cooking apples
- 2oz / 50 g brown sugar
- 2oz / 50 g unsalted butter
- 1/2 pt / 275 ml double cream
- 4 egg yolks
- 2oz / 50 g caster sugar
- 1 dsp cornflour
- 1/8 pt / 75 ml Calvados
- 1lb / 450 g sweet pastry (see page 124)
- icing sugar to finish

Method:

1. Roll out the pastry and use it to line a lightly greased 8 inch / 20 cm flan ring. Allow to rest in the refrigerator for about 30 minutes.

2. Line the flan case with foil and a layer of baking beans, and bake blind in a moderate oven for 25 minutes. Take the flan case out of the oven, remove the foil and beans, and return to the oven for another 10 minutes.

3. Peel and core the apples and cut each one into 8 segments.

4. Heat the butter in a frying pan and add the apples and brown sugar, tossing over a fierce heat until lightly caramelised.

5. Add the Calvados and allow to flame.

6. When the flames have died, arrange the apples in the flan case.

7. Whisk together the egg yolks, caster sugar, cornflour and cream, and pour over the apples.

8. Bake in a moderate oven Gas 5 / 375°F / 190°C for about 45 minutes.

9. Dust with icing sugar, and serve warm or cold.

Travelling in France one October, my car gave up on me. I got out and peered through the window of the "Bar Rio". A roughly spherical lady with a fine moustache opened the door suspiciously. I introduced myself as a chef, and suddenly it was as if I had mentioned the words "American Express?" to one of those hotel receptionists on TV. She beamed at me, and insisted that I stay to dinner.

The flavours of that dinner are engraved in gold upon my tongue. My final memory is of drinking Madame Rio's home-made Eau de Vie de Cerise - and her crunching the cherry stones in her nut-cracker teeth!

I woke the next day lying on a bench in the Bar Rio. I got up to stagger out and find a garage, and found a note on the table. Madame Rio was better than American Express! Her son was a local mechanic, and he had resuscitated the car while we had been busy drowning ourselves in Eau de Vie! It started first time and has run perfectly ever since!

Duck Livers with Balsamic Vinegar & Almonds

Affordable richness!

Page 44

Bulwinkle's Mackerel Brandade

An English version of a Provençal classic

Page 45

Guinea Fowl with Yellow Pepper Coulis

Complementarity of colour and of taste

Page 46

Right

Orange Bread & Butter Pudding

An English classic with a novel twist

Page 48

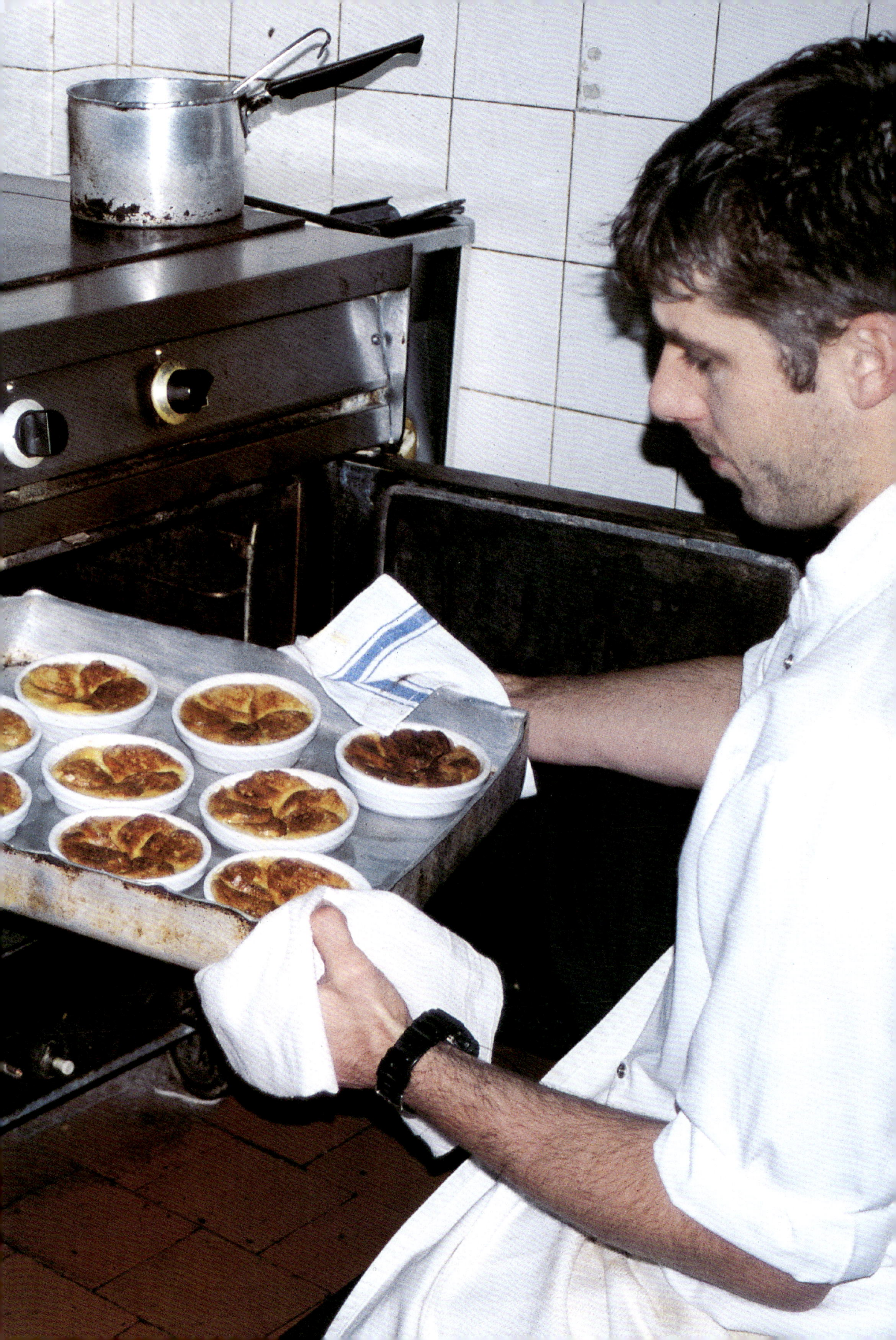

June

May was very beautiful. But then she proudly introduced Al to two older girls more beautiful still. He looked, amazed, from one to the other, and could not decide which was the more attractive. "Each seemed to outshine the other."

"These are my twin sisters, June and July", said May. "Perhaps they can help you better than I."

They were indeed very alike, but July had a slightly senior bearing, lending her beauty a solemn gravity. Whereas June was all youthful bubbles and smiles.

They led him, one on either side, to where a sparkling stream cascaded down over some rocks into a pool below.

Rillettes of Duck

Keep some of this as a standby in the fridge - equally good as a snack or starter

Serves 6

Ingredients:

    1 duck, or 4 duck legs
    salt and pepper
    4 fl oz / 110 ml vegetable oil (or duck or goose fat)

Method:

1. Bone out the duck and remove the skin.

2. Place the skin, bones and any fat in a moderate oven in a small pan.

3. Chop the meat roughly.

4. Strain the fat into a thick-bottomed pan, heat, add the meat and colour well.

5. Add the vegetable oil or equivalent and cover. Place in a moderate oven to stew for a couple of hours, until the meat is falling apart.

6. Drain the meat, place in a large bowl and flake well with a fork. Add a little of the fat to the meat, season well and leave to set.

7. Serve with warm potato salad as a starter, or crispy French bread as a snack.

In the Dordogne, my friend Champagne Charlie and I once befriended a local called M Magnanou. Charlie went on a poaching expedition with him, and landed them both in trouble with the local gendarme!

The next day, I was trying to prepare a meal. In theory, a chef never travels without his set of knives. But in practice, chefs are very bad at remembering things. Or at least this one is!

I was beginning to despair. Then there was a knock at the door. It was Mme Magnanou. She was furious about the poaching incident and wanted us to promise not to lead her husband astray again!

Suddenly, she stopped talking. She saw the pitiful sight of beautiful French poultry lying on the chopping board, about to be hacked up unceremoniously by a dull and blunted carving knife.

The kitchen door was closed, and a shady deal was done. Mme Magnanou let me have full access to her set of knives. I promised that there would be no more poaching expeditions. I felt like Judas. But everybody has his price!

Watercress Soup with Salmon Dumplings

Packed with goodness and flavour

Page 56

Jambonneau of Chicken

Chicken dressed as ham!

Page 57

Right

Rillettes of Duck

A French classic from the Tours and Anjou regions

Page 53

Rhubarb Tart Brulée

Reach for your blowtorch!

Page 61

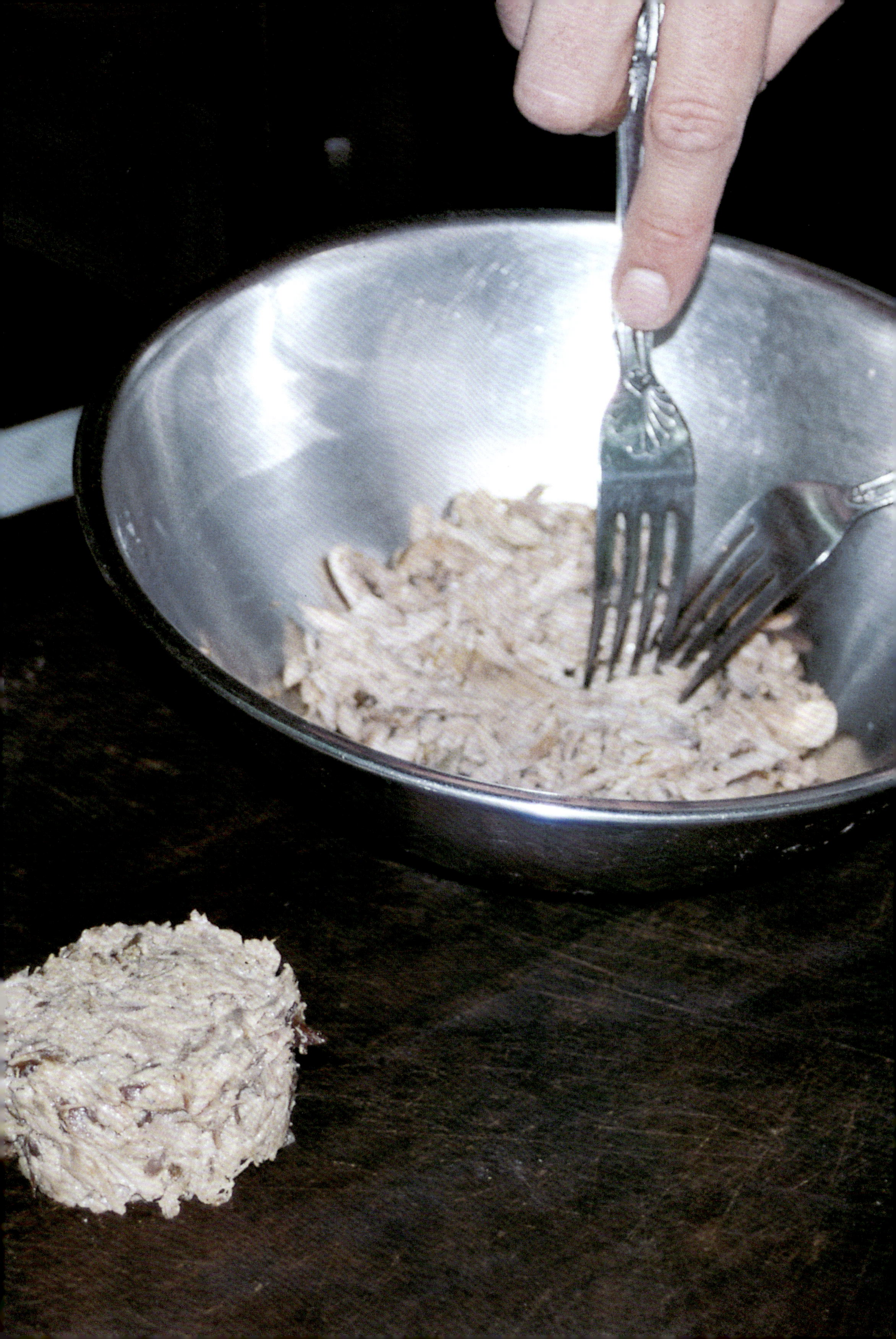

Watercress Soup with Salmon Dumplings

Light and fluffy balls of flavour in a smooth, nourishing soup

When my son was younger, he used to complain that he couldn't get to sleep. I asked him if he had tried counting sheep. He said that he had, but it didn't work.

So I said to him that that was because sheep were very easy to count, and they didn't do anything interesting. Why didn't he count fish instead?

I took him through to his room and told him that his mind was a vast playground of images. He didn't have to limit himself to boring old sheep. I asked him to close his eyes and imagine a refreshing, splashing stream cascading down the mountains, with huge silver salmon leaping upstream.

Then I asked him to imagine how the salmon swam further upstream to where the water was quiet and covered with green lily pads. Here they discovered fluffy warm duvets and pillows to wrap themselves up in and sleep after their long and tiring journey.

By now he was fast asleep. And I realised I had unwittingly created the idea for this soup from my ramblings.

Serves 6

Ingredients:

For the Soup:
2 oz / 50 g unsalted butter
2 oz / 50 g chopped onion
2 small cloves garlic, chopped
1 lb / 450 g potatoes, peeled and roughly chopped
1 small bunch watercress, 4 oz / 110 g approx.
3 pts / 1.7 l chicken or vegetable stock (see pages 117 / 120)
1 oz / 25 g plain flour
salt and pepper

For the Dumplings:
4 oz / 110 g salmon fillet
1 egg white
3 fl oz / 75 ml double cream
1 slice stale bread
4 fl oz / 110 ml milk
salt and Cayenne pepper

Method:

The Dumplings:

1. Soak the bread in the milk, then gently squeeze out the moisture.

2. Blend the fish in a food processor, add the bread and combine until smooth. Add the egg white and blend well, then turn the mixture out into a bowl and beat in the cream. Season with a little salt and Cayenne pepper, then refrigerate for 1 hour.

3. When the soup is almost ready, shape the mixture into small dumplings, using two teaspoons, and poach them for about 5 minutes in gently simmering salted water. Drain and keep warm

The Soup:

1. In a thick-bottomed pan, melt the butter and add the onion and garlic. Cook gently for 5 minutes without colouring.

2. Add the flour and cook without colouring for a further 5 minutes.

3. Gradually add the warmed stock, stirring until completely combined.

4. Add the potatoes and simmer for about 15 minutes, and add the watercress and simmer for a further 15 minutes. Liquidise the soup and pass through a medium strainer into a clean pan.

5. Bring back to the boil and skim the surface. Adjust the consistency with a little water if necessary and season to taste.

6. Divide the dumplings equally between six warmed soup bowls, and add the soup. Sprinkle with a few cut chives and serve immediately.

Chef's Tip: Adding the flour makes for a better consistency. But for those who are diet conscious or allergy-aware, it makes very little difference to the taste. Add 1 oz / 25 g potato if omitting flour.

Jambonneau of Chicken

A classic French method for stuffing chicken legs

Serves 4

Ingredients:

    4 large chicken legs,
        with the bone removed, but with the skin left on.
    1 small (about 4 oz / 110 g) breast of chicken,
        skinless and boneless
    1 tbsp chopped fresh tarragon
    1 tsp pink peppercorns
    1 egg white
    3 fl oz / 75 ml double cream
    1/4 pt / 150 ml dry white wine
    1/2 pt / 275 ml red wine sauce (see page 116)
    a few drops of lemon juice
    vegetable oil for cooking
    salt

Method:

1. Blend the chicken breast in a food processor until smooth, then add the egg white, tarragon and peppercorns and combine well.

2. Turn out into a bowl and gradually beat in the cream. Refrigerate for 1 hour.

3. Lay the boneless legs, skin side down, on a clean surface. Season lightly, and spread the filling evenly on each leg.

4. Roll up the legs tightly, and secure well with cocktail sticks.

5. Heat a little oil in a roasting tray, and colour the joints evenly all over.

6. Place in a moderate oven, Gas 5 / 350°F / 190°C, for about 45 minutes, until cooked through.

7. Remove from the roasting tray and allow to stand for 5 minutes. Remove the string or cocktail sticks and keep warm.

8. Discard the fat from the roasting tray, and add the white wine. Simmer for about 5 minutes, stirring to combine the sediment from the tray.

9. Add the red wine sauce, bring to boil and strain into a clean pan. Bring back to the boil, add a few drops of lemon juice and season to taste.

10. Place the chicken on warm plates and pour over enough sauce to cover them.

   Chef's Tip: This dish will keep well if made the day before. Leave the legs in a small container, cover with the sauce, cool and refrigerate. Make sure that the dish is re-heated thoroughly for at least 25 minutes before serving.

I have a friend who is a computer technician. He likes to spread harmless technology stories in the companies that he visits to see whether people believe them or not. He knows he's had a success when somebody in another company relates the story back to him, having heard it on the corporate grapevine.

His latest trick was to make a great show of straightening out the cables once he had fixed a computer system. He would explain that it was important to do this every month or so because of the nature of digital information, which, of course, is all ones and zeroes.

The zeroes can cope with bent cables easily, because of their rounded edges. But the ones sometimes get stuck because of their pointy shape, and can't get round the corners! To his glee, this story was reported back to him many times!

Well, I don't suppose he'll believe me, but jambonneau is a stuffed chicken leg. And it is so called because it looks like a miniature knuckle-end of ham.

Crab Cakes with Grain Mustard

A simple yet subtle combination

Page 66

Grilled Tuna with Béarnaise Sauce

Try this on a barbecue instead of steak

Page 68

Raspberry Mille-Feuille

Chef's love story: Part II

Page 70

Far right

White Chocolate Bavarois with Raspberry Coulis

Chef's love story: Part I

Page 71

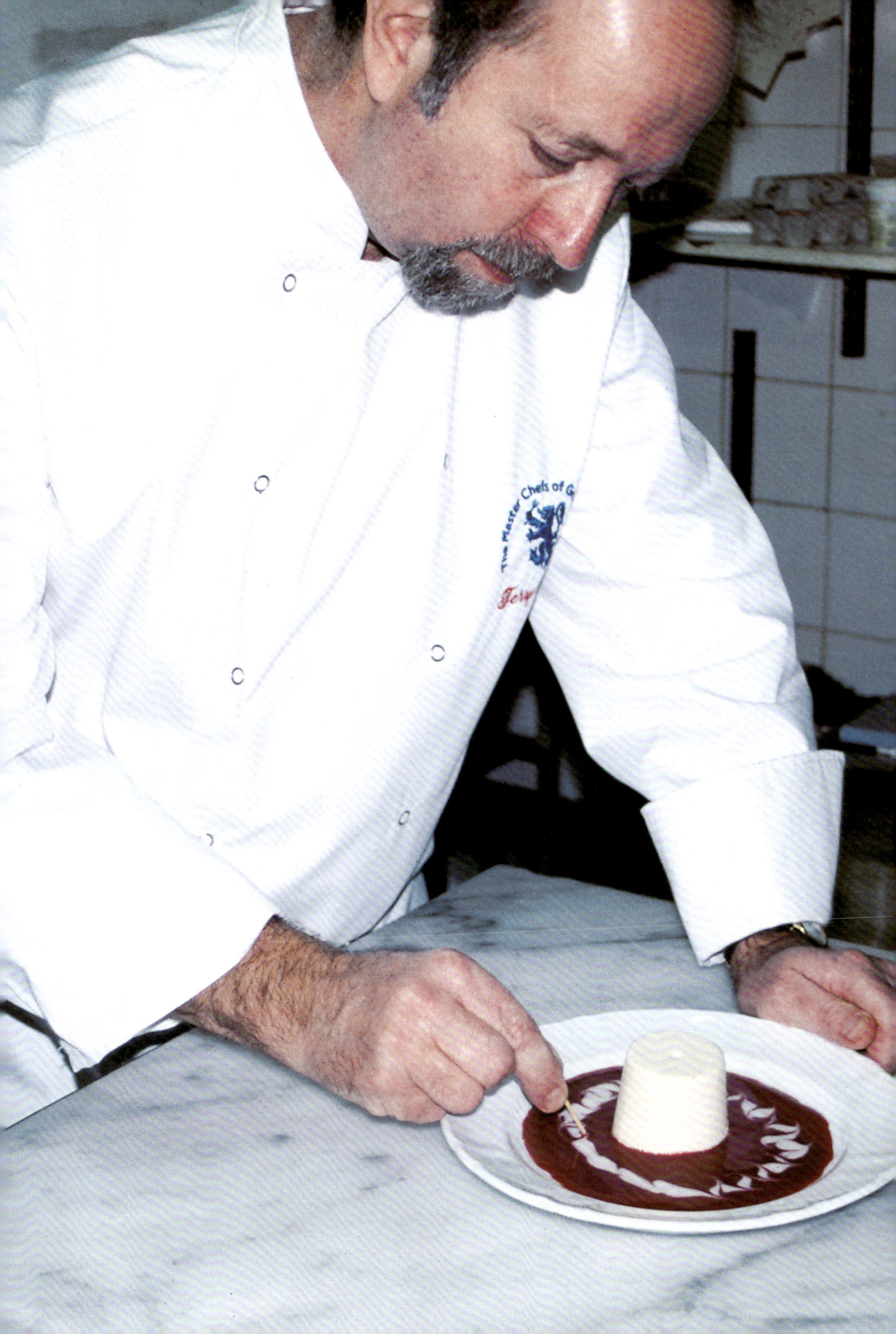
The Master Chefs of

Roast Monkfish with Garlic & Wild Mushrooms

Monkfish tail is extremely firm and meaty and easily filleted

My son and I once booked a fishing trip on the south coast. The boat belonged to a hoary old salt called Captain Bulwinkle. We asked him if we might catch any monkfish on our trip.

"Mebbe", he grinned wryly, "though I doubt if ye'd want to".

Bulwinkle told us how, at the tender age of fourteen, he had hauled a monster monkfish aboard his father's fishing vessel. This specimen resented being caught very much, and it thrashed violently around in the well of the boat to make sure everybody knew it.

It fixed its eye on the young Bulwinkle and went for him! He wedged the handle of a broom in its mouth, and in about thirty seconds it had chewed it up!

He found himself holding the brush jammed tight in the beast's maw and gazing into its eyes, and still its jaws kept working. Eventually somebody stunned it with a rock.

To this day, he will not eat monkfish. So here is a recipe for the rest of you!

Serves 4

Ingredients:

1 large monkfish tail: 2-2$^{1}/_{2}$ lb / 900-1125 g approximately
2 or 3 large cloves garlic, peeled and sliced
a few sprigs of fresh thyme
olive oil
salt and mill pepper
12 oz / 350 g chanterelles (or other available wild mushrooms)
2 oz / 50 g finely chopped shallots
a few drops of lemon juice

Method:

1. Trim the monkfish of all the skin and membrane. Wash, dry and tie the fish tightly to give a good round shape.

2. Heat a thick-bottomed ovenproof pan, add some olive oil and brown the fish, turning and seasoning it with salt and pepper as you go.

3. Make small incisions in the fish and press the slices of garlic in.

4. Sprinkle the fish with the fresh thyme (do not use dried thyme) and place in a hot oven for 20-25 minutes.

5. In the meantime, wash and dry the mushrooms and cook them in a pre-heated pan with olive oil, shallots and seasoning.

6. Add the cooked mushrooms to the monkfish and squeeze a few drops of lemon juice over the dish before serving.

Chef's Tip: This dish is superb when cooked outside on a Bar-B-Que.

Rhubarb Tart Brulée

Don't let anything stand between you and this dessert

Serves 6

Ingredients:

For the Tart:

8 oz / 225 g sweet pastry (see page 124)
1 lb / 450 g sliced rhubarb
2 oz / 50 g unsalted butter
6 oz / 175 g caster sugar

For the Topping:

3 oz / 75 g caster sugar
3 egg yolks
1/4 pt / 150 ml double cream
1 vanilla pod
3 oz / 75 g demerara sugar

Method:

1. Grease 6 individual tartlet moulds. Roll out the pastry to a thickness of about 1/4 inch / 5 mm and line the moulds with it. Leave to rest in a cool place for 30 minutes.

2. Line the moulds with baking foil weighed down with a few baking beans. Bake blind in a moderate oven Gas 6 / 400°F / 200°C for about 20 minutes.

3. Cook the rhubarb together with the butter and sugar in a thick-bottomed pan for a few minutes until just soft.

4. Pour the cream into a saucepan and bring to simmering point. Add the vanilla pod, simmer for 5 minutes and remove from the heat. Cream the caster sugar and yolks together, then pour the cream over the yolks, whisking continuously.

5. Remove the foil and beans from the moulds and divide the rhubarb evenly between them. Press down gently and evenly.

6. Cover each tartlet with custard and smooth the tops. Sprinkle the demerara sugar evenly over each tart and glaze under a very hot grill, or with a hand-held gas torch, until brown and crisp.

7. Turn out onto warm plates and serve with a little crème anglaise (see page 121).

When I make this dish, nothing gets in my way. I just have to finish it. But once my limits of ingenuity were severely stretched.

We had the builders in, and they were messing around with everything. I have a very hazy appreciation of how diaries work (I must get somebody to explain them to me) and I had arranged a lunch party for the same day!

Luckily, Roger the vicar was one of the guests, so divine intervention held off the inevitable until the end. Just as I was finishing the rhubarb tart brulées, however, the grill packed up.

But, as Roger will tell you, paraphrasing Romans: "...I am persuaded, that neither death, nor life, nor angels, nor principalities, nor powers, nor things present, nor things to come, nor height, nor depth, nor even the builders, shall be able to separate Terry from his rhubarb tart brulée!"

And so it proved. I seized an acetylene blowtorch from a surprised plumber who was doing unmentionable things to one of our radiators, and finished the desserts off with that.

Chicken Cooked in Ratatouille

More from the storehouse of Provence

Page 75

Vegetable Strudel

A vegetarian feast

Page 76

Strawberry Délice

Délice by name Délice by nature

Page 78

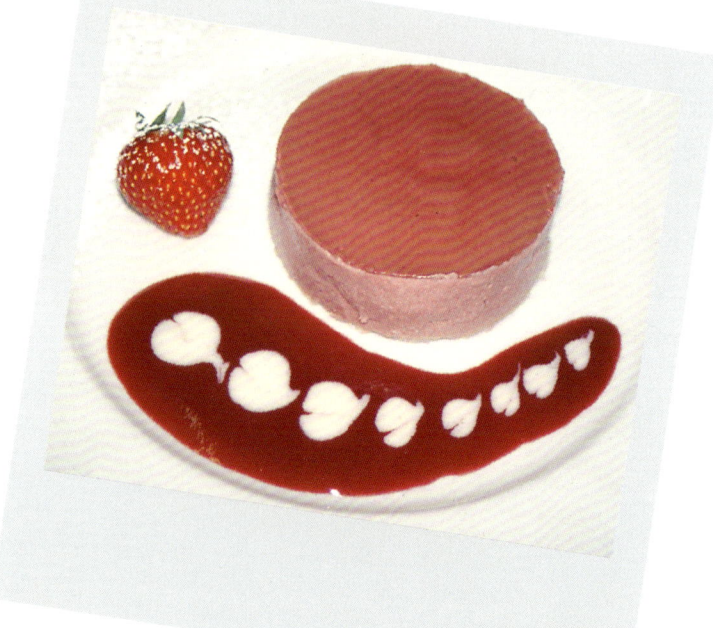

Right

Goats' Cheese & Red Pepper Tart

God for Harry, England and St George! (see story)

Page 73

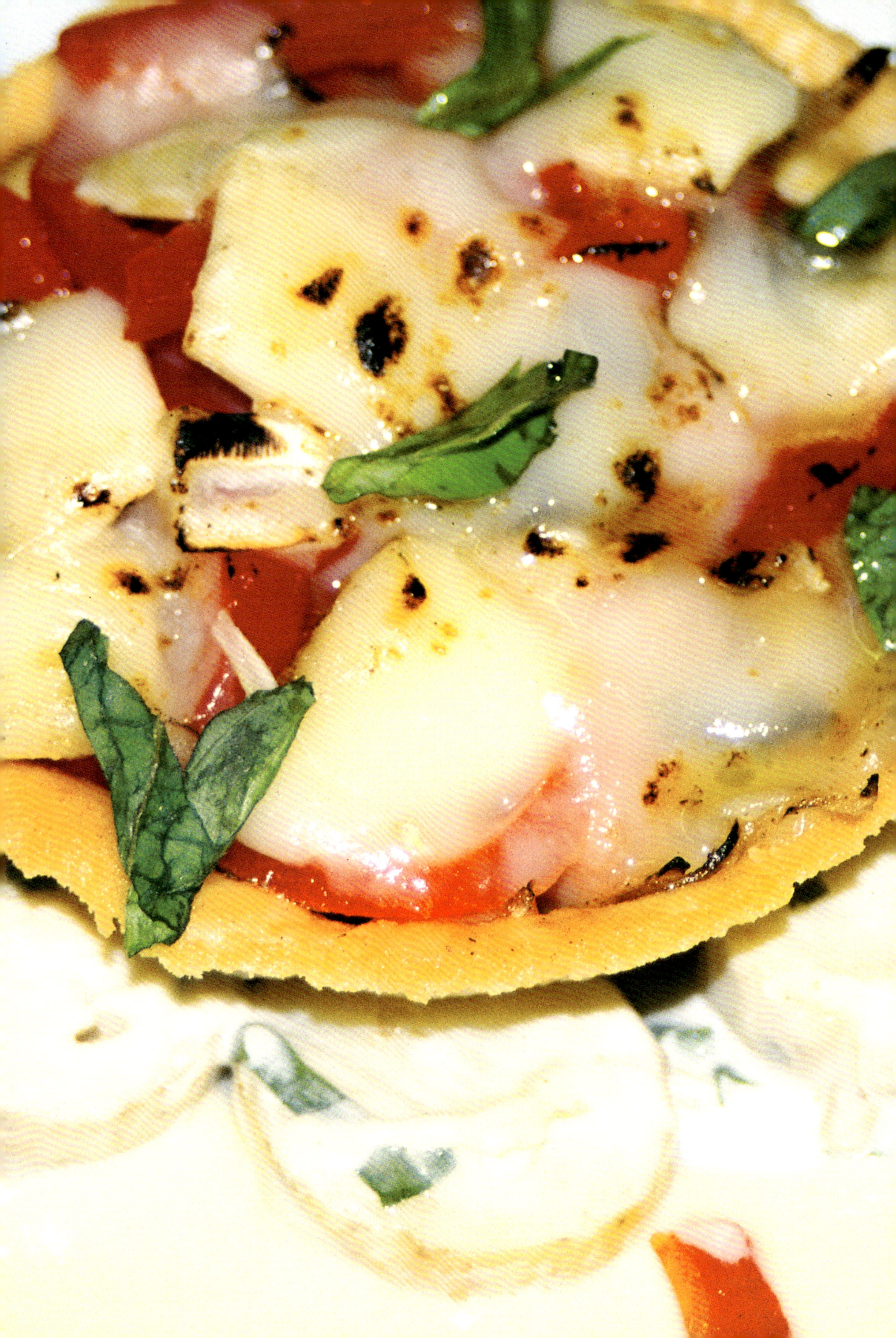

Coconut Parfait with Pineapple Compote

You can't make any mistake about the sunny nature of this dessert

I once visited the Caribbean island of Barbados. The flight was long and rough, and I fell into a deep sleep as soon as I checked in. I was rudely awakened at about midnight by a groping hand on my neck. When I felt it I froze. I thought my time had come. I remember wondering ridiculously whether, if I offered to cook the intruder a good meal, he would relent and not finish me off after all!

The intruder's groping became urgent. Then he spoke: "But...but, you're not my wife!"

The tone was almost plaintive, as if a special treat had been denied to an expectant child. But the content of what he said was undeniable. I rolled over, peered into the darkness, and congratulated the intruder on his powers of observation.

"Well, who are you then?"

"Terry Farr, who are you?"

His eyes almost popped. "You can't be Terry Farr. I'm Terry Farr!"

I had been given this couple's spare key by mistake. And I had been so tired I hadn't even noticed their suitcases in the room!

Serves 8-10

Ingredients:

For the Coconut Parfait:

1pt / 570 ml coconut cream

5 egg yolks

2 oz / 50 g caster sugar

5 leaves gelatine

7 egg whites

3/4 pt / 400 ml double cream

1/8 pt / 150 ml Malibu

For the Pineapple Compote:

10 oz / 275g fresh pineapple, cut into small 1/4 inch dice

1pt / 570ml water

4 oz / 110g granulated sugar

1 split vanilla pod

Method:

The Parfait:

1 Soak the gelatine in cold water.

2 Cream the yolks and sugar.

3 Bring the coconut cream to the boil, and add to the yolks, whisking continuously.

4 Return the mixture to a clean pan and cook gently, without allowing to boil, until the custard coats the back of the wooden spoon.

5 Drain the gelatine, and add to the custard, stirring until completely combined, allow to cool.

6 Fold in the lightly whipped cream, and the Malibu.

7 Fold in the stiffly beaten egg whites, carefully and pour into a 2 pt / 1.2 l terrine mould, lined with clingfilm.

8 Place in the freezer, overnight.

The Compote:

1 Make the syrup by simmering the water sugar and vanilla pod for 20 mins

2 Add the pineapple, bring to the boil for 2 minutes, then remove from the heat and allow to cool

To Serve: Remove the parfait from the mould, and cut into thin slices with a hot knife, and place on plates, spooning the compote around the outside.

July

"Your father", said July, "I seem to remember he liked fishing didn't he?"

Al jumped with surprise. "Yes. It was his favourite thing", he said. "How do you know? When did you see him?"

Her eyes misted over as she gazed into the pool. "Yes", she said. Her voice trickled from her lips like the silver droplets of the stream. "Long ago. Long, long ago. But look! Here is where he stood, I think."

They looked down, and there, sculpted deep into the grassy bank, were two footprints. Al placed his shoes within them, and suddenly a fishing rod of lithe and supple willow appeared in his hands.

Crab Cakes with Grain Mustard

Your guests certainly won't want to get away when you serve this as a starter

Serves 6-8

Ingredients:
1 lb / 450 g white crab meat
1 lb / 450 g mashed potatoes
2 tbsp mayonnaise
2 tbsp grain mustard
2 tbsp chopped spring onions
2 tbsp fresh white breadcrumbs
salt and mill pepper to taste
vegetable oil for cooking

Method:

1. Sift through the crab meat to remove any fins or shell. Mix all the ingredients except the oil and shape into little cakes.

2. Heat the oil in a thick-bottomed pan and then shallow fry the cakes. Drain on kitchen paper and serve on hot plates with a lemon butter sauce.

After staying with me for a short time several years ago, Champagne Charlie announced that he was "moving on". I asked why. The answer hung unspoken in the air. I nodded. With Charlie, there had to be a woman involved.

"I've brought something for you to cook", he said. He brought from his bag two fresh Cornish crabs.

"I was standing moping at the fishmongers", he began. "I saw these two chaps on the slab. They took me right back to childhood holidays in Cornwall when I used to go fishing for crabs off the end of the pier with some chopped squid on a hook and line. Eventually I would haul one up, with the squid in its claw."

"And I'm damned if it didn't come to me in a flash! By holding on to something unobtainable, the poor crab ends up boiled or potted or dressed and served up as somebody's lunch!"

"Well, Laura", I thought, "that will not happen to me. I'm going to see my old mate Terry for a spot of luncheon, and then I'm off!"

Avocado & Smoked Chicken with Poppy Seed Dressing

I've been doing this dish for 20 years and it's still popular!

Serves 4

Ingredients:

    1 large or 2 small breasts of smoked chicken,
      about 8-10 oz / 225-275 g
    2 firm, ripe medium sized avocados
    4 fl oz / 110 ml walnut oil
    4 fl oz / 110 ml vegetable oil
    1/2 tsp Dijon mustard
    1/2 tsp caster sugar
    2 fl oz / 50 ml white wine vinegar
    2 level tsp of poppy seeds
    salt and milled pepper

Method:

1. Make the dressing by whisking together the mustard, sugar and vinegar. Season lightly, then add the oils gradually, whisking continuously until completely combined. Add the poppy seeds and check the seasoning.

2. Remove the skin and trim the chicken if necessary. Carve, at an angle, into thin slices.

3. Cut the avocados in half, remove the stones and peel. Place them flat side down, and cut into thin slices.

4. Place a little tossed salad in the centre of the plates and arrange the avocado and chicken alternately in a fan on top of the salad. Spoon the dressing over and serve.

Chef's Tip: This dish can be produced more economically by using less white meat, shredding the dark meat and tossing it in with the salad.

I once went to a "silver break-up" party. The hostess was a friend of mine who likes her men lightly grilled and served up on a bed of guilt and remorse. (I hasten to add that I have never been the object of her culinary attentions!)

Every new relationship for her is a cause for celebration. And when it breaks up it is a cause for even greater celebration!

When asked about her logic, she cites Thomas Edison and his light bulb. After about 2,500 attempts to make a bulb that worked, a reporter interviewed him and asked why he didn't give up, as the idea was obviously a failure. He replied: "On the contrary, young man. I have successfully identified 2,500 designs that don't work!"

The rest is not just history, it shaped history! My friend was celebrating this break-up with special enthusiasm because it was the fiftieth design, by her reckoning, that she had identified that didn't work!

Grilled Tuna with Béarnaise Sauce

A barbecue dish with a twist in the tail

A barbecue is one of the simplest methods of cooking. Yet there are as many interesting recipes for food outside as there are inside. Life in the summer garden shouldn't be a string of carbonised sausages and cremated steaks.

Make sure that you prepare the barbecue correctly. Don't barbecue the food while the flames are still leaping from the firelighters. This has the doubly undesirable effect of cooking the outside of the food too quickly and of coating the food in the oily residues of paraffin combustion.

Firelighters are just that. Fire lighters. Once they have burnt out, the coals generate their own heat from the powerful combustion reaction taking place inside them. The heat is transmitted to the food by radiation and not by the direct contact of flame. The coals are ready when they appear grey and ashen on the surface.

This recipe is an interesting twist on barbecue food. It uses tuna steaks instead of beef. And why not? the main flavouring of Béarnaise sauce is tarragon - a classic herb for cooking with fish.

Serves 4

Ingredients:

For the Tuna:
4 x 5-6oz / 150-175 g fresh tuna fillets
1 tbsp olive oil
2 cloves crushed garlic

For the Béarnaise Sauce:
2 tbsp white wine vinegar
1/2 glass white wine
1 finely chopped shallot
10 crushed peppercorns
a few chopped tarragon stalks
3 large egg yolks
9 oz / 250 g melted unsalted butter
1 dsp chopped fresh tarragon leaves
a few drops of lemon juice

Method:

1. First, make the Béarnaise sauce. Boil and simmer the ingredients except the egg yolks, butter, tarragon leaves and lemon, in a shallow thick-bottomed pan until almost dry. Allow to cool slightly.

2. Add the yolks to the reduced liquid and whisk them over a low heat until light and aerated.

3. Whisk in the melted butter gradually then pass through a strainer into a clean bowl. Add the tarragon and lemon juice and season to taste. Keep warm until required.

4. Rub the garlic into the tuna and brush with oil. Grill the fish on both sides for about 10 minutes (or more if you prefer it well done). Season the fish while it is cooking (seasoning too far in advance draws liquid from the flesh and it will dry out and stick to the grill).

5. Serve with the Béarnaise sauce and salad.

Noisettes of Pork with Ginger & Spring Onion

Succulent pork with an oriental touch

Serves 4

Ingredients:

12 noisettes cut from a pork fillet, weighing about 1 1/4 lb / 500 g in total
1/4 pt / 150 ml white wine
1/4 pt / 150 ml double cream
2 oz / 50 g fresh ginger, finely grated
1 oz / 25 g chopped shallots
1 clove garlic, smashed
3 oz / 75 g spring onions, finely shredded
2 oz / 50 g unsalted butter
salt and mill pepper

Method:

1. Heat the butter in a thick-bottomed pan. Season the pork lightly and cook gently on each side for about 10 minutes in total.

2. Place the noisettes in a dish and keep warm.

3. Add the ginger, shallots and garlic to the pan and cook gently for a few minutes.

4. Add the wine and reduce by half, stirring to remove the sediment from the pan.

5. Add the cream, bring to the boil and pass through a fine strainer into a clean pan.

6. Bring back to the boil and add the spring onions. Reduce the sauce a little to thicken if necessary and season to taste.

7. Spoon the sauce over the noisettes and serve.

Do you remember the Tamworth Two? Of course you do. We shall remember them for as long as we remember the Magnificent Seven, the Birmingham Six, the Renault Five, the Petit Four and the Wealdstone Three!

(Actually, you may not remember the last group, but I certainly do. They were a family of three who loyally supported Friends during the dark days of the recession!)

The Tamworth Two were two wild boar who escaped from an abattoir. In a frenzy of anthropomorphism displaying the best characteristics of WWII escape veterans, they tunnelled under the perimeter fence and ran for their lives (literally) to the river. They jumped in and swam to the other side, (although pigs can't swim). Their anthropomorphism obviously didn't extend to studying Natural History! Then they made off into the sunset like the two legendary cowboys (Butch and Sundance) after whom they were named.

Here is a recipe for ordinary pork, which hopefully will not try to escape from your dinner table!

Raspberry Mille-Feuille

A dazzling party piece, sure to arouse the admiration of your guests

Long ago in France a chef went to work in the kitchens of a old château. The comtesse was a strikingly lovely woman, and the chef fell in love as soon as he saw her.

The chef plucked up courage to begin a series of secret assignations with her. She fell in love with him also and yearned for his food, seeing this as their secret route to communion with each other, even while she was in the company of her husband.

The affair was discovered and the chef was banished. But not before he was able to cook one final meal for his love. He coded a special message into the dessert for her.

He had often told her how his love for her filled the air of his kitchen as he cooked, and how he could fill a thousand leaves extolling his love. So he made the airiest of mille-feuilles for her, and filled it with the most passionately red fruit he could find.

The next morning he was expelled from the region, never to return.

Continued in next recipe.

Serves 4

Ingredients:

10 oz / 275 g raspberries
6 sheets filo pastry
1/2 pt / 275 ml double cream
1/2 pt / 275 ml raspberry coulis (see page 122)
1 measure (1/16 pt / 40 ml) Crème de Framboise
icing sugar for dusting
1 egg, beaten, for eggwash

Method:

1. Lay 3 sheets of filo pastry out on a clean surface and brush with eggwash. Lay the other 3 sheets on top and brush them also with eggwash.

2. Using a 2 inch / 5 cm pastry cutter, cut out 12 discs and place them on a baking sheet. Cook in a moderate oven Gas 5 / 350°F / 190°C for about 10 minutes until golden in colour. Remove from the oven and allow to cool on a wire rack.

3. Whip the cream and liqueur together until soft peaks form. Place a teaspoon of cream on each of the four serving plates and place a pastry disc on each one.

4. Take half the cream and pipe it onto the discs. Set half the raspberries on top and dust lightly with icing sugar. Set four more pastry discs on top and repeat the process with the remaining cream and raspberries.

5. Dust the remaining discs with icing sugar and glaze them under a hot grill. Allow to cool, and place them on top of the piles you have already prepared.

6. Spoon a little raspberry coulis around the side and dust the edges of the plates with icing sugar.

Chef's Tip: For extra effect, you can decorate this dish further by drizzling a little crème anglaise (see page 121) or double cream on the coulis and marbling with a cocktail stick.

White Chocolate Bavarois

You could easily fall in love over this velvet white dessert

Serves 8

Ingredients:
- 3/4 pt / 425 ml milk
- 3 oz / 75 g caster sugar
- 3 eggs, separated
- 1/2 pt / 275 ml double cream, lightly whipped
- 4 oz / 110 g white chocolate
- 2 leaves gelatine
- 1/2 measure Cointreau

Method:

1. Soak the gelatine in water.

2. Cream the yolks and the remaining sugar. Boil the milk and whisk into the yolks.

3. Return to the pan and cook over a low heat until the mixture coats the back of a wooden spoon. Be careful not to boil the mixture.

4. Remove from the heat, add the chocolate and gelatine and stir until smooth.

5. Strain the mixture and allow to cool.

6. When almost set, gently fold in the lightly whipped cream and the stiffly whipped egg whites.

7. Add the Cointreau and pour the mixture into a mould (or individual moulds if preferred). Allow to set in the fridge.

8. Turn out and decorate with whipped cream. Serve with a raspberry coulis or a dark chocolate sauce.

The banished chef from the previous recipe eventually ended up running an auberge in the foothills of the Alps, having changed his identity to avoid pursuit. But he still dreamed of his love every night.

One day, when he was nearing the end of his working life, his dream came true. His comtesse, now widowed, and having heard of his fame under his assumed name, came to sample his food. Seeing her through the kitchen window, she was as beautiful to him as she had ever been.

For dessert he sent out to her the following dish. She tasted it, and the white chocolate seemed to her like creamy snow melting on her tongue.

Such was the skill of her lover that she recognised his style as if it had been his handwriting. She pushed back the table, leapt up and burst through to the kitchen. Thenceforth the chef never ceased to write her letters of culinary love until the end of their lives.

August

A young man, dressed all in green, stepped out from the trees. "I am August", he said. "Let us see if we can catch anything."

So they sat by the pool, casting their lines into the water. Before long Al had a bite. He flipped the rod upwards and a fat fish flew through the air and landed wriggling on the bank.

"A fine meal", said August. "Let's go and see my brother, September. He's a great one for food. He'll tell us how to cook him."

And they walked back to where the other months were sitting by the fire.

Goats' Cheese & Red Pepper Tart

A feast for English eyes, and for more cosmopolitan taste buds

Serves 4

Ingredients:

8 oz / 225 g short crust pastry (see page 125)
4 oz / 110 g onions, peeled and sliced
1 clove garlic, peeled and chopped
2 large red peppers
4 slices goats' cheese (eg Ste Maure) 1 1/2 oz / 40 g each
olive oil
4 leaves fresh basil
salt and milled pepper

Method:

1. Roll out the pastry and use it to line four lightly greased individual tartlet tins. Allow to rest in a cool place.

2. Line the cases with foil and a layer of baking beans. Bake blind in a moderate oven for about 20 minutes.

3. Blacken the peppers under a very hot grill. Remove and place them in a covered bowl and allow to cool.

4. Scrape the skin off the peppers with a small knife, then cut them in half and remove the seeds.

5. Cook the onions and garlic in a little olive oil for about 15 minutes until lightly caramelised.

6. Remove the foil and baking beans from the tartlets and line the bottoms evenly with the onions.

7. Cut the peppers into strips and place them in the tartlets. Season lightly and place a leaf of basil and then a slice of goats' cheese on top of each. Drizzle a little olive oil over the tops.

8. Bake in a moderately hot oven, Gas 7 / 425°F / 220°C for 15-20 minutes until the cheese has melted and is lightly coloured. Serve warm, with a little warm salad of new potatoes.

---

*"There is a pleasure sure in being mad
Which none but madmen know."*

Dryden, The Spanish Friar.

"Hamlet: Ay, marry, why was he sent into England?

Clown: Why, because he was mad. He shall recover his wits there; or, if he do not, 'tis no great matter there.

Hamlet: Why?

Clown: 'Twill not he seen in him there. There the men are as mad as he."

Shakespeare, Hamlet.

I have some friends who are all English, and who meet every St George's Day to celebrate the fact. One of them once tried this recipe at Friends and now asks me to cook it every year for their celebration, because of its colours. It is more appropriate for late summer than St George's Day, but I think my two quotes say it all!

Soused Herrings

A simple classic recipe I picked up from a fisherman in a pub while on holiday

Serves 4-6

Ingredients:

    6 medium sized fresh herrings
    1 Spanish onion, finely sliced
    2 cloves
    1 tsp salt
    2 chillies
    12 peppercorns
    2 bay leaves
    1 blade of mace
    sufficient water and vinegar, in equal quantities, to cover the fish

Method:

1. Wash, scale, clean and fillet the fish. Discard the bones.
2. Roll up the fillets and secure with cocktail sticks.
3. Place in a baking dish and sprinkle the onions over. Season with salt.
4. Add the remaining ingredients and cover with the liquid.
5. Cover with a lid or foil, and bake for about 55 minutes. Allow to cool in the liquid and serve cold.

Here is a story from a friend who is an optician in the City of London. One of her customers, a Mr Soapstone, rang up and said he had forgotten his contact lens case and needed one urgently. He would send his messenger down to pick one up.

Time passed, and the messenger didn't appear. Then the phone rang, with a furious Mr Soapstone on the other end.

"What is the meaning of this? My messenger came to your shop and asked for a lens case. The person behind the desk looked blank. Then he rummaged around in a bin by the desk, and produced a black plastic container. "Here", he said, I suppose you could use this!"

Ellen walked out the front door and looked around. The opticians were next door to a photographic processing shop, and the opticians' sign hung between the two doors. The half-witted messenger had obviously gone through the wrong door and not realised his mistake!

Perhaps the messenger was slightly soused, or in need of brain food. Either way this recipe is appropriate!

Chicken Cooked in Ratatouille

It is worth taking some time to get to know this most Provençal of dishes

Serves 4

Ingredients:

For the Chicken:
1 x 3lb / 1.35 kg chicken, cut into small joints
1/2 pt / 225 ml white wine
olive oil
salt and pepper

For the Ratatouille:
6 oz / 175 g aubergine (diced)
6 oz / 175 g courgettes (diced)
2 oz / 50 g red peppers (deseeded and diced)
2 oz / 50 g green peppers (deseeded and diced)
2 oz / 50 g onions
2 small cloves garlic
8 oz / 225 g plum tomatoes
olive oil
1/2 pt / 300 ml Passata
salt and milled pepper

Method:
1. In a large shallow pan, heat a little olive oil, and cook the seasoned chicken on each side for about 5 minutes until they are a light golden colour. Remove the chicken and keep warm.
2. Discard the fat and de-glaze the pan, by adding the wine, and boiling whilst stirring continuously to loosen the sediment from the pan. Strain into a bowl and keep to one side.
3. Make the ratatouille as described below.
4. Place the chicken in an oven-proof casserole, add the ratatouille and the juices and the wine from the de-glazing.
5. Cook in a moderate oven, Gas 5 / 375°F / 190°C, for about 45 minutes.
6. Serve with rice, or garlic mash (see confit of duck on page 40).

The Ratatouille:
1. Blanch the tomatoes by plunging them first into boiling water for two minutes, and then into cold water. Peel the skin off and cut them in half and remove the seeds. Cut the flesh into a small dice.
2. In a thick-bottomed pan, heat a little olive oil and add the onions and garlic, and cook gently for about 5 minutes, without colouring.
3. Add the peppers and cook for another 5 minutes, then add the aubergines and courgettes, and cook for another 5 minutes.
4. Add the Passata and the diced tomatoes and bring to the boil, seasoning with salt and pepper.

Chef's Tip: This is effectively two dishes, so feel free to use the ratatouille for other purposes if you wish. If preparing this dish as a vegetable dish, place in the oven at step 6 for about 30 minutes.

Ratatouille is one of the most famous of Provençal dishes. It has spread from its birthplace in Nice, all over southeast France, and indeed across the world. Its popularity is perhaps surprising, as its name originally designated a stew of leftovers, and not particularly appetising ones at that.

Nowadays, of course, it has come up in the world. It can be seen dining at the finest tables, in very elegant company. Many roast meats are most proud to be seen with it, as are chicken (as here) and various types of fish. It is also served sometimes with scrambled eggs and omelettes.

It is full of the vegetable goodness of Provençal cookery, and heavy with the scent of the herbs of the region. Aubergines, peppers, tomatoes and onions all contribute to the powerful personality of this dish, and when it speaks, its voice is accented with overtones of garlic, thyme, bay leaves and rosemary.

Vegetable Strudel

A vegetarian treat, satisfying and full of flavour

M. Delorme, the Chef Saucier at the Connaught, once told me this story about his childhood. He had two sets of grandparents, both of whom doted on him (if you could believe him!)

One set lived in the country (let's call them Les Fermiers), and the other in the town (Les Villagers). Les Fermiers had a huge house with extensive grounds where they grew vegetables and flowers. Les Villagers lived in a small flat, with only a postage stamp garden.

The young chef used to take crops from Les Fermiers' garden to Les Villagers, which used to make them green with envy. Until one day he visited Les Villagers, and was given a small spade. He then went out and dug up a crop of a huge variety of vegetables!

Grandma Villager had spent the previous day burying vegetables from the market strategically throughout her tiny garden for the budding chef to dig up! Here is a dish he learned to make with the crops from Les Villagers' garden.

Serves 4

Ingredients:

- 8 oz / 225 g strudel leaves (filo pastry)
- 4 oz / 110 g red peppers, deseeded and cut into strips
- 4 oz / 110 g green peppers, deseeded and cut into strips
- 6 oz / 175 g small courgettes, cut into batons
- 4 oz / 110 g aubergine, cut into batons
- 2 cloves garlic, chopped
- 2 oz / 50 g onion, chopped
- 8 oz / 225 g tomatoes, skinned, deseeded and diced
- 8 oz / 225 g spinach, washed
- 1 tbsp basil, shredded
- 2 oz / 50 g wholemeal breadcrumbs, toasted
- olive oil
- unsalted butter melted
- salt and milled pepper

Method:

1. Blanch the spinach in boiling salted water for 2 minutes, then refresh under cold water.

2. Cook the peppers together in a little hot olive oil for 10 minutes. Cook the courgettes in the same way for 5 minutes, then do the same with the aubergine.

3. Heat a little olive oil in a thick-bottomed pan and cook the onion and garlic for about 5 minutes, without colouring.

4. Add the diced tomatoes and basil to the onions and garlic, and cook for a further 5 minutes.

5. Lay the strudel leaves out in four individual sections on a clean surface.

6. Lay a portion of spinach on top of each one, and cover with the onion and garlic. Season lightly with salt and pepper.

7. Place the remaining vegetables neatly on top and sprinkle with breadcrumbs.

8. Roll up the parcels, brushing the edges with melted butter to seal them. Brush the outsides with melted butter and cook on a lightly greased baking sheet in a hot oven Gas 8 / 450°F / 230°C for 20-25 minutes, until golden in colour.

9. Serve with some beurre blanc (see page 115) and chives, or a little tomato sauce made with vegetable stock.

Chef's Tip: To keep the pastry from drying out, keep it covered with a damp cloth whist waiting to use it.

Victoria Plum & Amaretti Tart with Blackberry Coulis

Luscious firm fruit with a crunchy biscuit topping

Serves 10 in 1 x 10 inch / 25 cm flan case

Ingredients:

For the Filling:
- 1 lb / 450 g firm Victoria plums
- 2 large tbsp thick clear honey
- 2 oz / 50 g raspberry jam

For the Topping:
- 4 oz / 110 g Ameretti biscuits
- 2 oz / 50 g dark brown sugar
- 2 oz / 50 g unsalted butter

For the Blackberry Coulis:
- 1/2 lb / 225 g picked and washed blackberries
- 2 oz / 50 g caster sugar
- 1/2 pt / 300 ml water
- a few drops of lemon juice

Method:

1. Roll out the pastry and use it to line a lightly greased 10 inch / 25 cm flan ring. Allow to rest in the fridge for 30 minutes.

2. Line the flan case with foil and a layer of baking beans, and bake blind in a moderately hot oven, Gas 7 / 425°F / 220°C for about 25 minutes. Remove the foil and beans, and return to the oven for another 10 minutes.

3. Spread the base with jam, and then fill with frangipane.

4. Halve the plums and remove stones. Place them, cut side down, onto the frangipane.

5. Bake in a moderate to hot oven for 30 minutes.

6. Crush the Ameretti biscuits and mix in the butter, making a "crumble".

7. Place the crumble mix on top of the flan, sprinkle with dark brown sugar and bake for a further 20 minutes to achieve the crunchy topping.

8. Meanwhile, make the blackberry coulis: bring the ingredients to the boil and simmer for 15 minutes. Pass through a sieve and adjust the consistency as necessary, adding lemon juice to taste.

9. When the tart is cooked, allow to rest for 10 minutes. Remove from the flan case and lightly dust with icing sugar. Serve with blackberry coulis.

Plums are a noble fruit. They have an enviable pedigree, going back to pre-Roman times. From their origins in Asia they have survived through the Roman Empire, the Crusades and the Renaissance to the present.

The most interesting period of their development occurred in 16th century France. Here they were actively cultivated and many new varieties were developed, such as the Goutte d'Or and the Plum de Monsieur (which was, incidentally, Louis XIII's brother's favourite). Thanks to these attentions we can now enjoy a great variety of descendants from these lines.

Depending on the variety, plums may be harvested any time from June until September. They thrive in English gardens, and I have more than I know what to do with most years!

This recipe is an excellent method of using up excess fruit. It uses Victoria plums, a very popular variety harvested in late August or early September.

Strawberry Délice

All the concentrated flavour of summer

Here is a special treat of a dish for my favourite young lady, Judy. She's only five, but she recently elevated me to the rank of Knight. Having been overlooked by Buckingham Palace, it was nice to be appreciated at last!

Judy is the daughter of a friend who lives in the West Country. She always needs recipes to use up her annual fruit harvest. Once she called in an almost hysterical state: "Terry you must come down. It's my damson trees. You have never seen such a crop. If you don't do something they will all go to waste!"

I raced off down the road (the M4 that is) to see them. I successfully managed to make a large quantity of damson ice cream with the fruit.

Then Judy appeared. "From now on we shall call you Sir Terry, because of you brave deeds in rescuing our damsons in distress!"

This recipe has nothing to do with damsons. But I promised Judy I'd get her into the book somehow!

Serves 8

Ingredients:

10 oz / 275 g strawberries
5 leaves gelatine
  (reserve one leaf for the glaze)
1/2 pt / 300 ml water
2 oz / 50 g caster sugar
3 large eggs, separated
1/2 pt / 300 ml double cream
1 slice Genoese sponge
  1/4 inch thick (to make the base)
1/8 pt / 75 ml Grand Marnier
a few drops of lemon juice
1/4 pt / 150 ml clear apple juice
1 tbsp strawberry jam

For the Genoese Sponge:

4 eggs
4 oz / 110 g caster sugar
4 oz / 110 g plain flour
2 oz / 50 g unsalted butter, melted
a few drops of vanilla essence

Method:

1. Soak the gelatine in cold water. Cream the egg yolks and sugar. Boil the water and add to the yolks, whisking continuously.

2. Return the mixture to the pan and cook gently without boiling, stirring continuously, until the mixture coats the back of a wooden spoon.

3. Remove from the heat and add 4 leaves of the drained gelatine, stirring until dissolved. Add the strawberries and leave to cool until lukewarm.

4. Blend the mixture in a food processor, and pass through a fine strainer into a large bowl.

5. Lightly whip the cream, and fold into the mixture. Beat the egg whites until they form stiff peaks and carefully fold them in. Add half the Grand Marnier and a few drops of lemon juice to taste.

6. Place an 8 inch mousse ring on a cake board, and place the sponge in the bottom. Sprinkle the remaining Grand Marnier over the base and pour the mixture in. Smooth the top with a palette knife and refrigerate overnight.

7. To make the glaze, boil the apple juice and jam, add the leaf of gelatine, and strain into a clean bowl. Allow to cool slightly. Brush over the surface of the délice.

The Genoese Sponge:

1. Whisk the eggs, vanilla and sugar together in a large bowl over a pot of hot water, until the mixture is very light and airy.

2. Sift the flour into the mixture, folding in carefully. Gently fold in the butter.

3. Grease and lightly flour an 8 inch / 20 cm cake tin, and put the mixture in.

4. Bake in a moderately hot oven, Gas 6 / 400°F / 200°C for 30-45 minutes.

5. Allow to cool on a cooling tray. Wrap in clingfilm until required.

September

September had many ideas about how to cook the fish. He had a long coat with many pockets, from which he drew out bundles of herbs and ripe vegetables. The fish was wrapped tightly in the last green leaves of summer and roasted in the ashes.

At length the fish was pulled out from the fire and the leaves split open. The aroma of the herbs floated heavenwards, and they all sat down to eat the best food that Al had ever tasted.

And, strange to tell, there was plenty to go round, and even some left over.

Green Bean & Tarragon Soup

An excellent dish to use up the last green beans of summer

I once attended a performance of "Waiting for Godot". The play in which nothing happens. And then happens again. It has been called an example of "Absurd Drama". I can't think why!

It all comes down to whether you regard that as a concept worth conveying to an audience. At the time I thought it wasn't. But the resonance with cookery has since struck me. You don't "do nothing" when cooking. But you often deal with very slow and subtle changes.

The character of Estragon (French for Tarragon) inspired this dish. Watching the antics of him and Vladimir was about as eventful as sitting down and watching a bunch of tarragon growing beside some runner beans all summer!

So if Godot ever turns up at Friends, I'll serve him this soup. But I'm, not waiting. We have a strict no-shows policy!

Serves 4

Ingredients:

2 pts / 1.2 l chicken or vegetable stock (see pages 117 / 120)
2 oz / 50 g chopped onion
2 oz / 50 g chopped celery
8 oz / 225 g trimmed and chopped runner (or other) beans
1 bouquet garni
2 cloves garlic, chopped
1 dsp freshly chopped tarragon
1 oz / 25 g butter (chilled)
salt and a few drops of lemon juice

Method:

1. Place the onions, garlic, celery and beans in a thick-bottomed pan. Heat the stock and add it to the other ingredients together with the bouquet garni. Bring to the boil, skim and simmer for 25-30 minutes.

2. Remove the bouquet garni and add the tarragon. Blend the liquid until smooth, and strain through a sieve into a clean pan.

3. Bring to the boil again, and adjust the seasoning and consistency, whisking in the cold butter if desired. Add a few drops of lemon juice to taste and serve with crusty French bread and croutons.

Crabmeat Sausage with Grain Mustard & Brioche Crumb

A visually and gustatorily exciting combination

Serves 4

Ingredients:

For the Sausages:
6 oz / 175 g picked white crabmeat
3 oz / 75 g fillet of sole
2 egg whites
2 oz / 50 g brioche crumbs
2 oz / 50 g chopped tarragon
1/2 pt / 275 ml double cream

For the Garnish:
chopped fresh chives
deseeded and diced tomatoes

To Serve:
Lightly toasted brioche

For the Sauce:
1/4 pt / 150 ml white wine
1/4 pt / 150 ml white wine vinegar
1 oz / 25 g chopped shallots
1 tsp crushed peppercorns
4 oz / 110 g hard unsalted butter (diced)
1 tbsp grain mustard (moutarde de Meaux)
a few drops of lemon juice

Method:

The Sausages:

1. Prepare a bowl over ice, and in a separate bowl process the sole to achieve a smooth purée. Add the egg whites gradually during the processing until completely combined.

2. Place the mixture in the bowl over ice and beat in the cream gradually. Fold in the crabmeat, tarragon and most of the brioche crumbs. Season.

3. Take four squares of clingfilm and pipe or spoon the mixture into them. Roll into sausages and seal. Poach the sausages for about 15-20 minutes and leave to stand.

The Sauce:

1. Reduce the white wine, vinegar and shallots until syrupy in consistency. Whisk in the butter a little at a time over a gentle heat.

2. Strain into a clean pan. Add most of the mustard and the lemon juice. Adjust consistency as necessary with a little water.

To Serve:

1. Remove the clingfilm from the sausages. Place on a lightly greased baking tray, brush with a little mustard and sprinkle with a few brioche crumbs.

2. Place under a hot grill for a few minutes until lightly coloured. Remove from the heat and place on four plates. Dress with the mustard sauce, sprinkle with diced tomato and chives and serve with lightly toasted brioche.

Many years ago, we had a family holiday in the Norfolk seaside town of Cromer, justly famous for its crabs. We had befriended one of the local fishermen. One day he took me and my son (aged 5 at the time) out sailing.

Suddenly, the wind changed, and we realised we were being driven onto an alarmingly close, craggy, lee shore! Frantic activity broke out. We wrestled with the sails and lowered them out of the wind. Our friend tried to start the outboard motor, but it wouldn't take. As I looked in dismay at the motor, partially dismantled, I heard a voice: "Has anybody got a pencil sharpener?"

I turned to see my son waving a pencil while standing precariously atop the cabin. Just then, our friend managed to start the motor. We started laughing, partly with relief, and partly at the incongruity of my son's request. His idea had been to write a "HELP!" message and throw it overboard in a bottle! We arrived home safely, and had Cromer crabs for lunch!

Crabmeat Sausage with Grain Mustard & Brioche Crumb

You've never had sausages like this before!

Page 81

Wild Boar Medallions & Rösti

Watch it doesn't get up and charge!

Page 84

Summer Pudding

The bridge from summer into autumn

Page 88

Far right

Halibut in Vermouth with Black Noodles

A visual and gustatory feast

Page 85

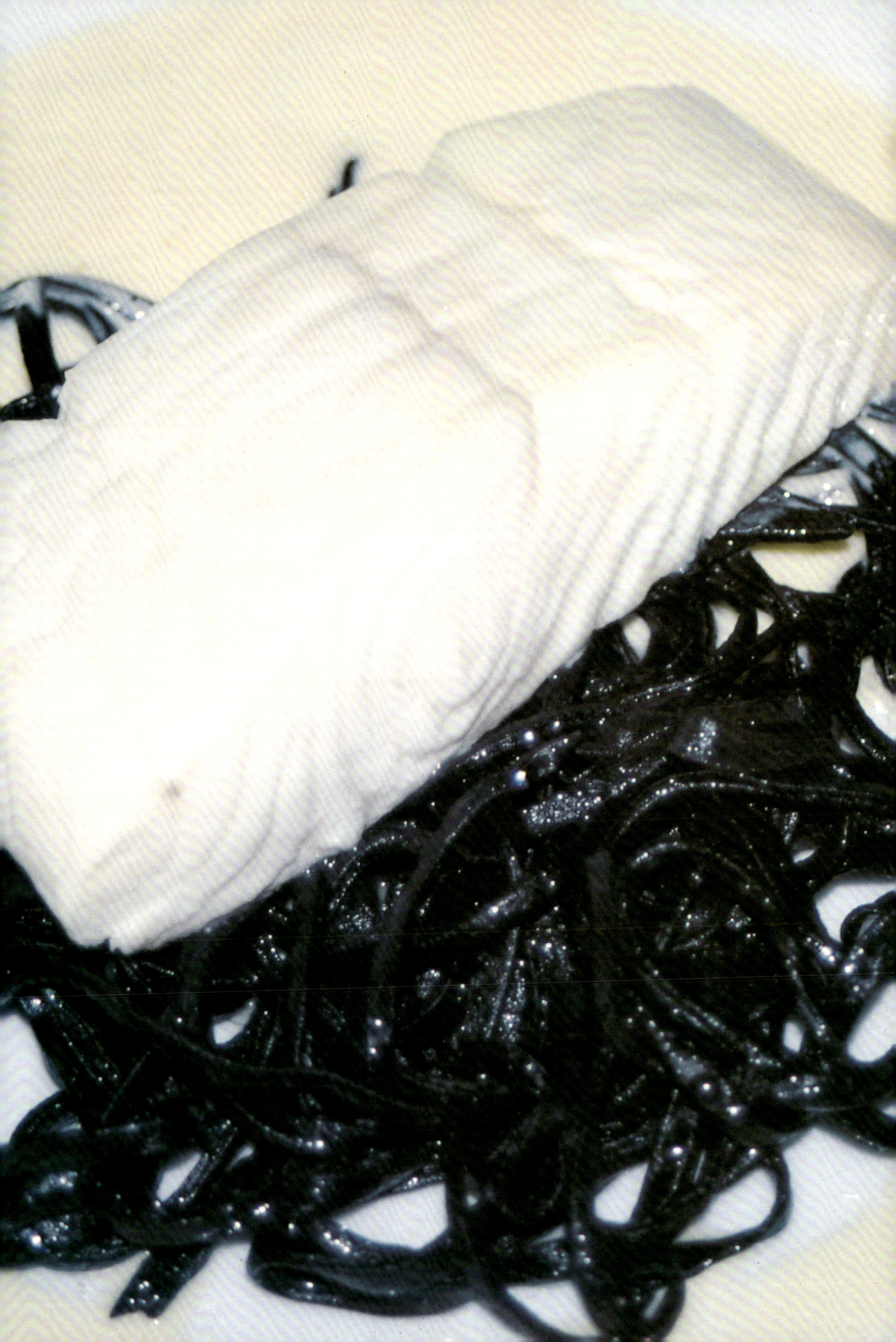

Wild Boar Medallions & Rösti

Medallions of Wild Boar with Juniper and Rösti

My grandfather Hugo liked nothing better than hunting wild boar, except perhaps cooking and eating them! He used to show me a pair of boar's tusks when I was a boy. I would always beg him to tell me how he had won them.

He had been out wandering in the forest. He was trying to learn English and he had with him a huge copy of Shakespeare. He sat down beneath a tree to read "As You Like It", imagining himself off with Rosalind and Celia in the Forest of Arden.

Suddenly he was disturbed by a huge wild boar, snorting and pawing the ground. He leapt up as it charged. Maintaining all his sang froid in the face of the bête noire, he choked it by stuffing his Shakespeare down its throat. Then he cut off its head and carried it home.

As a child I loved this story. Only later did I discover that the same legend surrounds the origin of the Boar's Head as a festive meal. Dare I think my grandfather had been telling "porkies"?

Serves 4

Ingredients:

12 oz / 350 g trimmed loin of wild boar
1/2 pt / 300 ml dry red wine
6 juniper berries, crushed
1 bay leaf
1 sprig fresh thyme
2 cloves garlic, crushed
vegetable oil for cooking
1/4 pt / 150 ml red wine sauce (see page 116)

For the Rösti:

4 large potatoes, about 1 lb / 450 g each (boiled in their skins)
salt and pepper
vegetable oil for cooking

Method:

The Boar:

1. Cut the boar into 8 equal slices, then flatten them firmly with a meat bat or hammer, until you have medallions about 1/4 inch thick.

2. Place the medallions in a shallow dish, adding the wine, juniper berries, herbs and garlic.

3. Cover with clingfilm and leave to stand in a cool place to marinate for 8 hours.

4. When you are ready to cook, drain the meat and season lightly. Cook the medallions in hot oil in a shallow frying pan for about 3 minutes on each side. Remove them from the pan and keep warm.

5. Discard the oil from the pan, and add the wine and other ingredients of the marinade.

6. Bring to the boil and simmer for about 10 minutes until reduced by half.

7. Add the red wine sauce and bring back to the boil. Season to taste and pass through a fine strainer.

8. Place the medallions on warm plates, spoon the sauce over the meat, and serve with the rösti.

The Rösti:

1. Drain and cool the potatoes, then peel and grate them into large strips.

2. Heat the oil in a large frying pan and add the potato, season and toss or stir until it starts to colour.

3. Press the potato down in the pan, allow to brown. and turn the cake, browning the other side.

4. Turn out onto a warm dish and serve.

Chef's Tip: When turning the rösti, turn it out onto a lightly greased dish and slide it back into the pan to preserve its shape.

Halibut in Vermouth with Black Noodles

Visually striking, this dish shines out like a black pearl!

Serves 4

Ingredients:

For the Fish:
- 4 x 5oz / 150 g halibut fillets
- 1/8 pt / 75 ml dry Vermouth
- 2 oz / 50 g unsalted butter
- 1/8 pt / 75 ml fish stock (page 118)
- 1/2 pt / 300 ml double cream
- 1/2 a lemon
- salt and pepper

For the Black Noodles:
- 4 oz / 110 g strong flour
- 1 egg, and 1 egg yolk
- 1 tsp olive oil
- 1 tsp squid ink
- semolina for dusting
- a pinch of salt

Method:

The Fish:

1. Lightly season the fish and poach in the stock and wine until just cooked. Cooking time depends on the thickness of the fish, but fillets 1/2 inch thick should take about 20 minutes.

2. Remove the fish from the stock, and keep warm.

3. Boil the stock to reduce by half and add the cream.

4. Reduce further by 1/3, and whisk in the butter. Add a few drops of lemon juice and season to taste.

5. Pass the sauce through a fine strainer into a bowl, and cover with cling film until required.

The Black Noodles:

1. Sieve the flour and salt into a bowl, and make a well in the middle.

2. Mix the eggs, oil and ink together and pour into the well.

3. Gradually mix the eggs into the flour to make a smooth dough.

4. Cover with a damp cloth and leave to stand for 30 minutes.

5. Dust a work surface lightly with semolina, and roll out the dough very thinly.

6. Pass through a pasta machine, or cut into thin strips and leave to dry.

7. To cook, plunge into plenty of boiling salted water for a few minutes. The pasta will rise to the top when cooked. Drain and toss in a little butter. Place the noodles on warm plates and place the halibut on top. Spoon the sauce over and serve.

Chefs Tip: When cooking the pasta, put a little oil in the water. This stops the pasta from sticking together.

Continued from page 44.

Champagne Charlie's teeth encountered two small pearls. To find one is very rare. But two is unheard of! He looked at his companion through the candlelight. She was so beautiful with her darkly shining eyes and wickedly smiling mouth...It was meant to be! He would propose, show her the pearls, and set them in gold for an engagement present! But just then a waiter upset a glass of wine over the table. They jumped up in surprise. The table was quickly mopped down, but the moment had passed.

"Didn't you propose later?" I asked. By way of answer he took out a twisted piece of paper, and opened it up to reveal two tiny pearls. "I'm a confirmed bachelor, Terry. That evening put the wind up me. I always carry these with me now to remind me not to lose my head!"

Out of sympathy for his feelings we went straight on to the main course!

Hot Vichysoisse with Smoked Salmon & Chives

Excellent hot or cold

Page 96

Partridge Pudding

A true English game pudding

Page 97

Sea Bass with Caramelised Fennel

A recipe worthy of this highly-prized fish

Page 98

Far right

Hazelnut Meringue Gateau

Crisp and light

Page 99

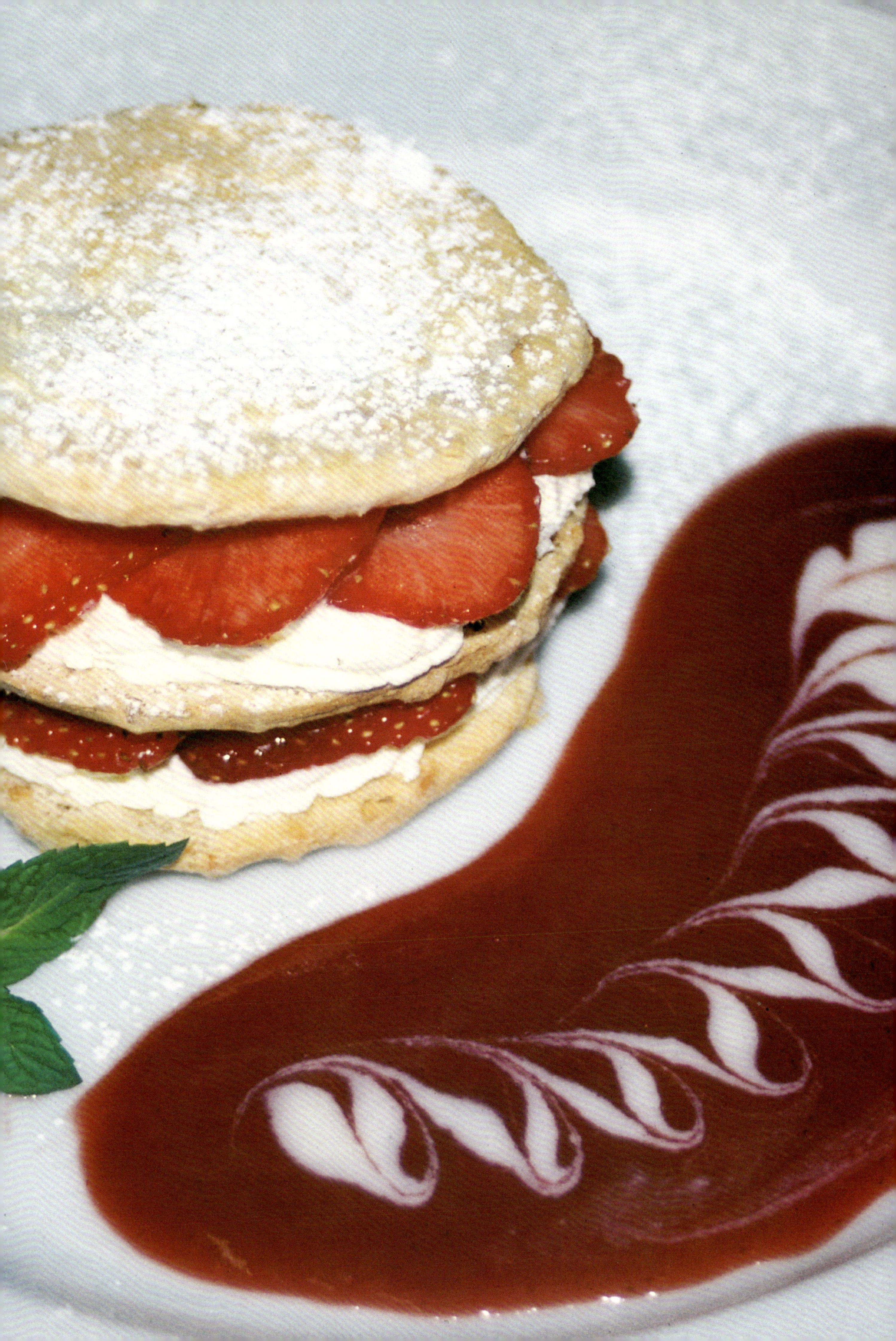

Summer Pudding

An ideal desert for the last of the summer fruits

This dish tells the story of the change of seasons. The basic ingredients brim with the goodness of late summer. But the ripe, juicy berries are tinged with musky mixed spice, foreshadowing the season of mist and woodsmoke, and the warmth of the Christmas festival deep in the frosty heart of winter.

The sad thing about it is that it is so popular in the restaurant that there is never any left for me to eat secretly between bouts of service. (Honestly, you wouldn't believe the things that chefs survive on in the kitchen!)

So I started making a second pudding to eat at home. But generally, by the time I get home, the locusts that I affectionately call my family have eaten that as well.

We chefs are nothing if not resourceful. I now make a third pudding. A very small one for me to eat all on my own in private. You might call it "Last of the Summer Puddings!"

Serves 6

Ingredients:

    1 lb / 450 g soft fruit (e.g. blackberries, raspberries, strawberries, blackcurrants)
    1 tsp mixed spice
    2 apples, peeled and grated
    sliced white bread with crusts removed (enough to line a suitable bowl)
    6 oz / 175 g caster sugar
    1/4 pt / 150 ml water

Method:

1. Pick the fruit and wash well. Leave to drain.
2. Bring the water to the boil and add the sugar.
3. Add the fruit and simmer gently until cooked. Do not overcook. Add spice according to taste. (This greatly enhances the fruit flavours).
4. Line the bowl with bread, without leaving any gaps.
5. Add the fruit and cover with more sliced bread.
6. Place a small plate on top and weigh down with a cup of water, in order to press the pudding slightly.
7. When completely cold, refrigerate for 24 hours.
8. Turn out, and serve with clotted cream and a sprig of fresh mint. Any remaining juice can also be served separately.

Chef's Tip: The presentation can be enhanced by making individual puddings, although it does take longer.

Clafoutis aux Cerises

Another classic regional French speciality

Serves 4

Ingredients:

For the Clafoutis:
9 oz / 250 g cherries, pitted
1½ oz / 40 g butter, melted
2 eggs
3½ oz / 90 g caster sugar
pinch of salt
2 oz / 50 g flour
4½ fl oz / 125 ml milk
½ fl oz / 10 ml Kirsch

For the Sauce:
4 dsp lemon juice
4 dsp lime juice
1 dsp honey
2 oz / 50g unsalted butter

Method:

The Clafoutis:

1. Whisk together the eggs, sugar, flour and salt, then whisk in the milk and Kirsch.

2. Butter an earthenware dish and arrange the cherries in it. Pour over the mixture and bake for 40 minutes at Gas 4 / 180°C / 350°F for 40 minutes. Allow to cool slightly and dust with icing sugar.

The Sauce:

1. To make the sauce, bring the lemon juice, lime juice and honey to the boil. Cut up the butter into small pieces and whisk it into the sauce. When it has emulsified pour it over the clafoutis and serve.

Clafoutis comes from the Limousin region of France. It is a typical example of the French paranoia about their culture. We have all heard about the government's attempts to preserve the integrity of the language. Thus when you use a TV remote control you do not "zap", you "saute-chaîne". In English is made up of so many others that we just don't care. If we purified English we would have to throw out the Greek, the Latin, the Danish, the German, The Mediaeval French, the Norse, the Indian and the American words and there would be nothing left!

The inhabitants of Limoges are as jealous about their clafoutis as the French are about their language. When the Académie Française defined it as "a sort of fruit flan", they insisted the definition be changed to "cake with black cherries". Similar arguments have happened in the past about bouillabaisse and other traditional dishes.

You'd have thought they would have enough on their plates just cooking. But no! They have to define and argue about what they are cooking as well!

Grilled Goats' Cheese with Celery & Walnuts

Ever wondered how to get that grilled effect

Page 103

Lime Tart

Gives a refreshing zing to your taste buds

Page 106

Butterscotch Brulée

Probably my all-time favourite dessert

Page 107

Right

Spinach Gnocchi

If only they'd had them in France '98....

Page 104

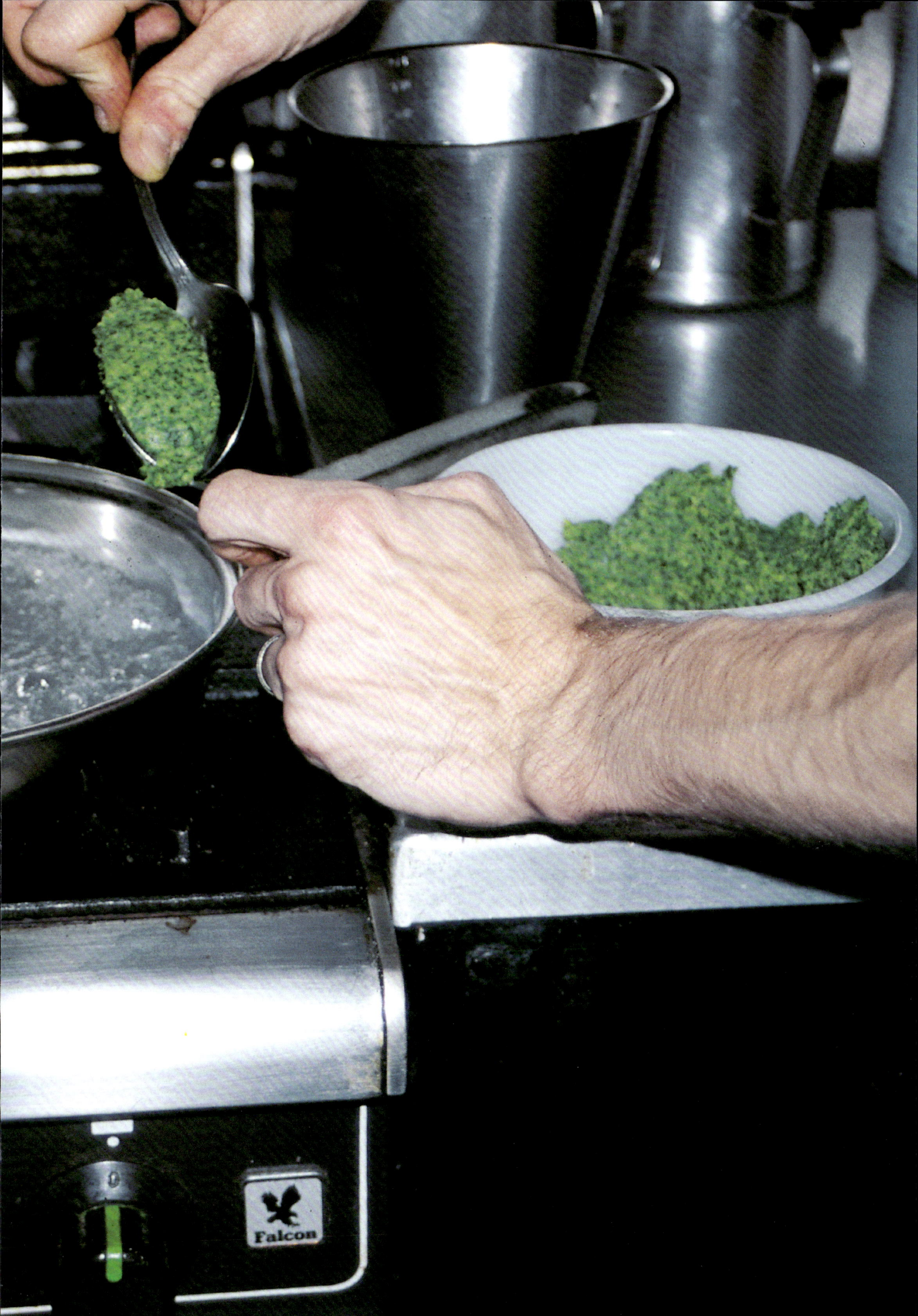
Falcon

October

Then October stepped forward. She had a full, voluptuous figure, and her complexion was like russet apples, her lips like shining chestnuts. She took a handful of leaves from her pocket. Al could see that they were all colours from green through golden yellow to brown.

She looked at each one closely, and Al could see that they were covered with spindly, crabbed writing.

As she finished reading each one, she tossed it to the jaws of the wind, which snatched it hungrily away, and chased it rolling across the countryside, catching and snagging in the hedgerows as it went.

Terrine of Lobster & Sole with Pistachio Nuts

A light and fluffy terrine with an original twist

Serves 8-10

Ingredients:

- 3/4 lb / 350 g fillets of Dover sole, trimmed and minced
- 8 oz / 225 g diced lobster meat, preferably uncooked
- 3 oz / 75 g pistachio nuts, blanched and skinned
- 2 egg whites
- 6 fl oz / 175 ml double cream
- 1 oz / 25 g lobster coral (if available)
- salt and Cayenne pepper

Method:

1. Line a 2 pt / 1.2 l terrine with clingfilm.

2. Blend the sole, egg whites and coral (if used) in a food processor until smooth. Turn out into a bowl set in ice and beat the cream in gradually.

3. Fold in the lobster and pistachio nuts and season with salt and Cayenne pepper. Turn the mixture into the terrine and cover with clingfilm, silver foil and the terrine lid.

4. Leave to stand in the fridge for one hour, then remove and cook in a bain-marie in a moderate oven Gas 5 / 375°F / 190°C for 55-65 minutes. Test with a thin-bladed knife, which should come out clean when the terrine is cooked.

5. Leave to cool and refrigerate overnight before serving.

Once while staying at The Cleeve House in North Devon, I met a lobster fisherman in a pub. He had invented an electronic lobster pot. When the pot was full, it lit a lamp attached to a buoy. With a pair of binoculars, he could tell whether to go out to investigate the pots. But one day he pulled up a message in a bottle instead of a lobster: "Dear Fisherman, thanks for the tasty bait. But down here you miss a plate of fish and chips. Could you arrange it? Yours, Larry (the Lobster)."

Over the next few days the notes requested more extravagant food, until Larry's wife, Libby, asked for Champagne and caviar. Fed up with being a culinary delicacy, she wanted to eat some.

The local teenagers were responsible. They had taken to raiding his high tech pots and making a nice profit around the local restaurants. So he went back to the old method. His electronic pot had taken all the fun out of it anyway. Like opening your presents before Christmas!

Roast Suprême of Pheasant "Grand Mère"

This was almost Champagne Charlies's Nemesis!

Page 111

Roast Loin of Lamb Stuffed with Dried Exotic Fruits

A completely different approach to this festive meal

Page 112

Chestnut Charlotte

A luxurious end to the year

Page 114

Far right

Scallops & Bacon with Honey & Sesame

A novel partnership of land and sea

Page 110

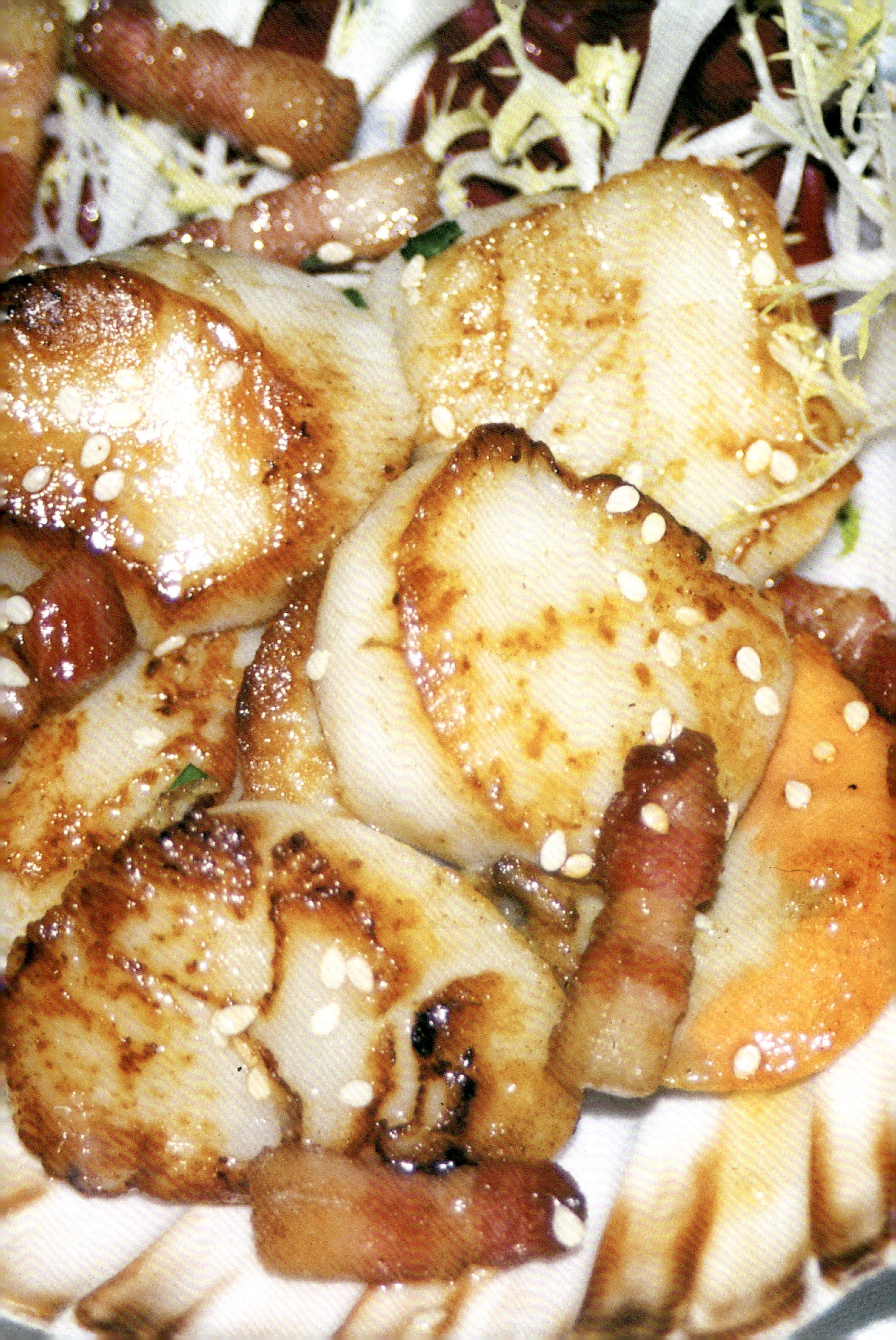

Hot Vichyssoise with Smoked Salmon & Chives

A subtle combination of potato and fish, with the mild onion flavours of leeks and chives

Serves 4

Ingredients:

- 2 oz / 50 g whites of leeks, washed and chopped
- 2 oz / 50 g onions, chopped
- 2 pts / 1.2 l chicken or vegetable stock (see pages 117 / 120)
- 2 oz / 50 g unsalted butter
- 1 lb / 450 g potatoes, peeled and chopped
- 4 oz / 110 g smoked salmon, cut into thin strips
- 1/4 pt / 125 ml double cream
- 1 tbsp finely cut chives
- salt

Method:

1. Heat the butter in a thick-bottomed pan and add the onions and leeks. Cook gently for about 5 minutes, without colouring.
2. Warm the stock and add it to the pan. Bring to the boil and add the potatoes.
3. Simmer for about 30 minutes. Liquidise and pass through a fine strainer into a clean pan.
4. Bring back to the boil. Skim any fat from the top, stir in the cream and season to taste.
5. Divide the smoked salmon equally between the warmed soup bowls, and pour in the soup.
6. Stir the soup to distribute the salmon, sprinkle the chives on top and serve at once.

Chefs Tip: Vichysoisse is classically served chilled, and indeed this recipe can be. If you want to serve it chilled on a hot summer's day, add the smoked salmon when the soup is cold.

In my younger days I was a great Jazz fan. There was a crowd of us who used to go to all the Jazz clubs in the sixties. One of our number was very small and baby-faced. So we always used to hide him in the middle when trying to gain entry to clubs, for fear of his being excluded as too young. We used to call him Snippet.

Well one day a couple of years ago Snippet himself walked into Friends Restaurant. He looked at me and said, "I bet you don't remember me". And I'm afraid I didn't, it had been so long ago.

He booked a table for 12 for lunch the following week. And imagine my surprise when he and his wife turned up, not with ten friends, but with their ten children! His wife is even smaller than he is, and had the nickname "Fraction" before he ever met her. Now they are collectively known as "Snippet, Fraction and the Recurring Decimals"!

Snippet's favourite soup was always vichyssoise. So here is my version of it.

Partridge Pudding

A good old-fashioned pudding for hearty appetites

Serves 4 - 6

Ingredients:

- 2 partridges (older birds)
- 4 oz / 110 g lean stewing steak
- 4 oz / 110 g field mushrooms, quartered
- 2 sprigs fresh thyme
- 1 clove garlic, smashed
- 1 tbsp fresh chopped parsley
- 3/4 pt / 500 ml chicken stock (see page 117)
- 1/4 pt / 150 ml red wine
- 8 oz / 225 g suet pastry (see page 126)

Method:

1. Roll out the suet pastry to 1/4 / 5 mm inch thickness. Use two thirds of it to line a well-greased 2 pint bowl (the other third is for the lid).

2. Remove the breasts from the birds and cut them in half. Cut the beef into 1/2 inch / 1 cm dice.

3. Put all the meat in a mixing bowl and add the flour, mushrooms, seasoning and herbs. Mix well and place the mixture in the lined bowl. Add the wine and enough stock to cover the mixture.

4. Roll out the remaining pastry and cover the pudding, pinching the sides well to seal it. Cover with greaseproof paper and a pudding cloth and tie tightly.

5. Steam for 3 hours in a steamer or covered saucepan, topping up the water as necessary.

6. When cooked, serve with braised cabbage and garlic mash.

This one is for my friend Steve, a true Norfolk country boy. Once while we were walking through a Norwich shopping centre, a brightly coloured 7-foot chicken walked past. It was advertising a new fast food outlet.

A few months later Steve called me urgently to visit him again. When I arrived, the door was answered by a brightly coloured 7-foot red-legged partridge! "How do you like it, Terry?" asked Steve (for it was he).

I was dumbstruck. I sat the partridge down and asked it to explain. "If you can sell chicken as fast food", reasoned Steve, "you can sell game as fast food. It's much tastier, it's in plentiful supply in Norfolk and I'm going to see my solicitor this afternoon to sign the contract for a shop lease!"

I telephoned the solicitor and cancelled the appointment. Steve needs protection sometimes. He really does! So thanks to me, the world will have to wait a bit longer for Grouse Nuggets and the Norfolk Fried Partridge Family Bucket. May I present the following "slow food" partridge recipe instead!

Sea Bass with Caramelised Fennel

Sea bass roasts extremely well, and is complemented admirably by the slight aniseed flavour of the fennel

Serves 4

Ingredients:

4 x 5 oz / 150 g pieces of fillet of sea bass, descaled but with skin left on
4 small bulbs of fennel, shredded
$1/8$ pt / 75 ml white wine
$1/8$ pt / 75 ml white wine vinegar
2 oz / 50 g unsalted butter
1 tsp brown sugar
$1/2$ a lemon
olive oil
salt and milled pepper
$1/4$ pt / 150 ml beurre blanc (see page 115)
1 tbsp chopped chives

Method:

1. Heat the wine, vinegar, butter and sugar together in a shallow pan and add the fennel.

2. Boil gently for about 25 minutes, until the liquid has evaporated and the fennel is slightly firm but caramelised. Add a few drops of lemon juice, and season to taste. Keep warm.

3. Brush the fish with olive oil and season lightly. Place in an ovenproof dish, skin side up. Cook in a moderate oven, Gas 6 / 400°F / 200°C for about 20 minutes. Do not overcook the fish, as it can become dry.

4. Heat the beurre blanc and add the chives. Season to taste.

5. Place the fennel in the centre of the warm plates, and set the fish on top. Pour the beurre blanc around the outside of the plate and serve at once.

Chef's Tip: The key to the success of this dish is the absolute freshness of the fish. This is true of all fresh fish recipes as a rule.

Once while on holiday on the south of England I was indulging in one of my favourite forms of tourism: visiting the pubs! You can normally find a salty old fisherman propping up a bar who will tell you about his adventures.

When I met old Harry, he was showing off a fine pair of sea bass. He was taking them home for his wife to cook for dinner. As we talked, he became morose. He said that some days when he caught nothing, he just felt the fish were laughing at him.

"These for instance." He indicated the sea bass. "I got 'em from the fishmonger. I mean what kind of fisherman goes to the fishmonger?"

He turned to go. As he reached the door, I noticed he had forgotten his fish. "What about these?" I called.

"Oh yes. Chuck 'em over will you?" I did so.

"Thanks Terry." he said. "I never lie to the wife. Now I can tell her I caught two beautiful sea bass today!"

Hazelnut Meringue Gateau

A spectacular confection of hazelnuts & light meringue

Serves 4

Ingredients:

For the Meringues:
2 egg whites
4 oz / 110 g caster sugar
2 oz / 50 g chopped roasted hazelnuts
$^1/_2$ pt / 300 ml strawberry coulis (see page 122)
icing sugar to finish

For the Filling:
8 oz / 225 g strawberries
5 fl oz / 150 ml double cream
1 oz / 25 g caster sugar
1 measure Kirsch

Method:

The Meringues:

1. Whisk the whites to a soft peak, then add the sugar and continue whisking until stiff peaks form. Fold in the chopped nuts.

2. Pipe the meringue through a plain tube onto a non-stick baking sheet, making eight equal circles.

3. Cook the meringues in a moderate oven, Gas 4 / 350°F / 180°C for about 10 minutes, until lightly coloured. Then turn the oven to its lowest setting for about 2 hours until they are dried out. Allow to cool.

The Filling:

1. Whisk the cream, sugar and Kirsch to a stiff peak, and spread equal amounts on each meringue.

2. Slice the strawberries and place them on top of four of the meringues.

3. Turn the other four meringues over on top of the strawberries. Place them on plates and serve with a little strawberry coulis and dust lightly with icing sugar.

Chef's Tip: You may find it helpful to draw circles on cooking parchment using a glass or large pastry cutter, and placing it on the baking sheet.

M. Delorme, chef saucier during my days at the Connaught, was very particular about his Crêpes Suzette. And one day it came to his attention that the Chef de Rang in the restaurant was not making them correctly! So he went and had a typically Gallic remonstration with the Head Chef, the legendary M. Toulemon. Many gesticulations later, M. Toulemon called the Head Waiter.

Nothing would then do but the Head Waiter must assemble the entire Restaurant Brigade, again with much exclamation and waving of arms. And for what purpose? Why, to watch M. Delorme deliver a lesson in how to create the perfect Crêpe Suzette! We all stood in perfect silence while the master gave of his wisdom.

It was a humbling experience. It always reminds me how even experienced chefs need to revisit their basic techniques constantly to avoid complacency and staleness creeping in.

This recipe may appear more complex than Crêpes Suzette. But all recipes are simply longer or shorter chains of basic techniques strung together.

Warm Fig & Wild Honey Tart

A rich and warming autumnal fruit tart

I have a dear friend from Bakewell. When I first met her I said: "So you're a Bakewell Tart!" Then I suddenly realised this was a situation where an idea appears new to one person, but is embarrassingly old to another. She must have heard that hundreds of times!

It was like that old Monty Python sketch about Mr Smoketoomuch. He introduces himself to somebody, who replies "well, you'd better cut down a little". Mr Smoketoomuch looks baffled, but gradually pieces the joke together. "Yes, that's rather good", he muses, "I must remember that".

The Pythons had taken my "Bakewell" situation, and turned it on its head. This shift in perspective is essential in all creativity, from humour to cookery. This is how new recipes are born.

This tart began life as a Bakewell Tart, but turned into something quite different along the way!

Serves 10 (in one 10 inch / 25 cm flan case)

Ingredients:

1 lb / 450 g sweet pastry (see page 124)
8 oz / 225 g frangipane (see page 123)
10 large fresh figs
  (preferably the purple variety)
2 large tbsp thick clear honey
2 oz / 50 g raspberry jam

Method:

1. Roll out the pastry on a lightly floured surface. Line the flan case with pastry, allow to rest for 30 minutes.

2. Line the flan case with foil and a layer of baking beans, and bake blind in a moderately hot oven, Gas 7 / 425°F / 220°C for about 25 minutes. Remove the foil and beans, and return to the oven for another 10 minutes.

3. When cooked, spread the base with raspberry jam.

4. Spread the frangipane over the jam.

5. Trim and halve the figs and press them, cut side uppermost, into the frangipane.

6. Bake in a moderate to hot oven Gas 6 / 400°F / 200°C for 30 minutes.

7. Cover the flan with the honey and cook for a further 10 to 15 minutes. Allow to rest for 10 minutes before cutting and serving with crème anglaise.

November

Then November darted out from the undergrowth. She was lithe and handsome, like a huntress. Unerringly, she let loose an arrow from her quiver and pinned one of the leaves to a tree as it passed by upon the wind.

As she did so, the snow began to fall again, and soon the earth was but a memory once more. She walked to the tree and retrieved the leaf. She stood reading it and nodding with satisfaction. Then she turned to an old man sleeping beneath the tree, and shook him.

"Here, old man, a message for you."

Kipper Pâté with Whisky

Inspired by my early days at the Connaught

Serves 4

Ingredients:
- 4 kippers
- 1 measure whisky
- 2 oz / 50 g full fat cream cheese
- 1 oz / 25 g unsalted butter, melted
- 1 medium onion, sliced
- a few drops of Worcestershire sauce

Method:

1. Bake the kippers and onions in the oven with a little water until just cooked.
2. Fillet the kippers carefully and remove the skin.
3. Blend the fillets, onion and melted butter, together with the cream cheese, whisky and Worcestershire sauce in a food processor until smooth.
4. Spoon into an earthenware dish and refrigerate overnight.
5. Serve with fresh crusty French bread.

I know a cat of very regular habits called Kipper. Every morning he leaves his house at 8.00, and returns at 5.00 for his tea. His owner finds it a very satisfactory arrangement.

But one day Kipper went missing. His owner went mad looking for him for about a week. Then one morning she was walking down her street and saw Kipper sitting in the front window of somebody else's house!

She was most hurt that Kipper could so easily betray her for another owner. She marched up to the front door and rang the bell, ready to demand an explanation.

There was no answer, so she peered through the window. Through the curtains she could see that that the house was being redeveloped. Kipper had got locked in last time the builders were there.

His owner was so pleased to have him back that she came to Friends and ordered a whole takeaway portion of this recipe, which happens to be Kipper's favourite. He can't eat too much of it though, or the whisky sends him to sleep!

Grilled Goats' Cheese with Celery and Walnuts

Goats' cheese goes extremely well with nutty flavours and salads

Serves 4

Ingredients:

- 4 slices goats' cheese, 1 1/2 oz / 40 g each (Ste Maure or similar)
- 4 oz / 110 g celery, peeled and cut into thin strips
- 3 oz / 75 g shelled walnuts, roughly chopped
- 1/2 lb / 225 g curly endive
- 6 fl oz / 175 ml walnut oil
- 2 fl oz / 50 g white wine vinegar
- 1 tsp Dijon mustard
- 1 level tsp caster sugar
- 1 egg, beaten, for eggwash
- 2 oz / 50 g plain flour for dusting
- salt and milled pepper

Method:

1. Make the dressing by whisking together the mustard, sugar and vinegar. Gradually add the oil, whisking continuously until completely combined.

2. Toss the endive, celery and walnuts together in the dressing and season to taste.

3. Place the sliced goats' cheese on a lightly greased baking sheet. Dust with flour and brush with eggwash.

4. Place the cheese under a hot grill and allow to brown lightly, without melting too much.

5. Cover the plates with salad, place the cheese on top and serve at once with a little crusty bread.

Chef's Tip: You can make criss-cross markings with a hot poker on the cheese to give the grilled effect. Do this after dusting with flour, but before applying the eggwash.

Another story from Ellen, who used to be an optician in the city of London. Many high-ranking officials from major corporations used to come to her to get their eyes fixed. One such was Mr Smallbone.

Ellen was completing some records when Mr Smallbone walked in. She indicated the testing chair, which was very new and "high-tech", standing quite a way off the ground, like a dentist's chair.

"All right, Mr Smallbone", she said, "just hop up on the testing chair over there."

She finished completing the records, and turned to deal with her new patient. But then had to postpone the examination for about five minutes while she stopped laughing.

Mr Smallbone, respected captain of industry, had literally hopped up on the chair. He was standing on it, crouched like some demented billy-goat on a craggy outcrop.

This recipe is dedicated to Ellen as it reminds me of the dangerous job she has to do!

Spinach Gnocchi (Gnocchi Verde)

A traditional Italian dish made with semolina and spinach

Serves 4

Ingredients:

2 oz / 50 g fresh watercress leaves
4 oz / 110 g baby spinach
$^1/_2$ oz / 10 g chopped parsley
2 tsp each of chopped tarragon and marjoram
2 oz / 50 g each of ricotta and curd cheese
$1^1/_2$ oz / 40 g semolina
1 egg, beaten

Method:

1. Wash and blanch the watercress and spinach in boiling salted water for 2 minutes and drain well.

2. Chop the spinach and watercress finely and mix together in a bowl with the herbs.

3. Blend the two cheeses and the egg in a food processor and turn out into the bowl, folding into the chopped vegetables and herbs. Stir in the semolina and allow to stand in a cool place for 30 minutes.

4. Shape the mixture with two dessert spoons into quenelles (small oval shapes) and drop into a pot of simmering salted water. When the gnocchi rise to the surface they are cooked and ready to serve.

5. Drain the gnocchi well, place in a hot serving dish, grate some fresh Parmesan over the top and serve with ciabatta or garlic bread.

I am a very keen football fan. And I was very pleased to hear that they were going to appoint a team chef for the summer '98 World Cup campaign. Obviously they would choose somebody from near Wembley, because of the strong associations with 1966. . And they would probably cast their net as wide as the Harrow area, perhaps even Pinner...

As they say on the terraces, Terry, "In your dreams!"

As we all know, Roger Narbett got the job. I had intended this recipe as a last-minute suggestion for him. I was that sure they were going to go all the way this time! Sadly, as we all know, it was not to be. And I don't suppose Roger gets round to reading my columns in any event!

Anyway, if our boys had gone all the way in France, I would have recommended a dish like this for the night before the final. It is full of carbohydrate, the perfect athletic "loading" food. Ask any marathon runner.

Salmis of Wild Duck

A dense, rich game stew, which will in fact go very well with (game) chips

Serves 4

Ingredients:
- 2 wild duck (preferably older mallard)
- 8 shallots, chopped
- 3 carrots, chopped
- 3 cloves garlic, chopped
- 4 rashers smoked streaky bacon
- 1 bay leaf
- 1 sprig of thyme
- 1 pint duck or chicken stock
- 2 oz / 50 g butter
- 2 oz / 50 g plain flour
- 1 large glass of port
- 8 green olives, stoned
- salt and mill pepper

Method:

1. Rub seasoning into the ducks all over and wrap the bacon around them. Roast in a hot oven for about 30 minutes. Remove, drain well, cut into jointed portions and place in a casserole.

2. Add the chopped shallots, carrots and garlic to the duck juices in the roasting pan and roast for 15 minutes. Strain off the fat. Melt the butter into the roasted vegetables, add the flour and combine well. Cook gently on the hob for about 8 minutes.

3. Add the port and stock gradually and bring gently to the boil, stirring continuously. Cook the sauce for about 20 minutes and then strain over the duck portions.

4. Add the herbs, cover the dish and cook in a moderate oven Gas 6 / 400°F / 200°C for 45-55 minutes, or until the duck is tender.

5. Add the olives and cook for a further 10 minutes. Remove the bacon and serve.

Following Steve's abortive foray into the fast food market (see Partridge Pudding), there remained some loose ends. Like the twenty brace of wild duck he had ordered (and paid for) in anticipation of his first week's trading!

They had been destined for the centrepiece of his menu: the Double Duck Dinner Deal. Two pieces of mouth-watering wild duck breast served in a soft toasted bun with red wine sauce, regular chips and "megamug" of soft drink. All for £3.00!

"Chips?" I cried incredulously.

"Yes, Terry. Game chips. Thinly sliced deep fried celeriac".

This mollified me slightly. Game chips are actually very good, and easy to make. But the fact remained - we had to get rid of all these ducks. I ended up preparing a huge Salmis of Wild Duck, and a large quantity of game chips.

And so it was that Steve and I realised his fast food dream, just for one day, from a freezing stall in Norwich market. And from the way it went, I wondered whether his idea had not been so bad after all!

Lime Tart

A refreshing variation on the classic lemon tart

I was once on holiday with my family on the south coast. From the first day we found ourselves unable to escape from another family who seemed to share one brain cell between them.

For example: we were sitting one day waiting for an excursion bus to take us on a sightseeing trip. The son of the family was about to take a picture of us with his camera. It was a single-use camera where you take the whole unit back to the shop for processing. It was called a "Weekender".

Suddenly the father called out: "Stop Tommy. Let me have that camera." Tommy gave it to his father, who took out his mobile phone and rang a number written on the side of the camera. He spoke to someone, and seemed satisfied. Then gave the camera back to Tommy.

"It's all right, Son. I was just checking that it's OK to use it on a weekday."

The fellow-guests may not have been that bright, but the cookery was. Here is my version of one of the hotel's desserts.

Serves 8

Ingredients:
    6 limes
    12 oz / 350 g caster sugar
    6 large eggs
    1/4 pt /150 ml double cream
    1 lb /450 g sweet pastry (see page 124)
    3 oz / 75 g apricot jam
    icing sugar to finish

Method:

1. Grate the zest of the limes into a bowl, then squeeze the juice through a strainer into the same bowl.

2. Break the eggs into a separate bowl and add the sugar. Whisk together until smooth. Add the zest and juice.

3. Lightly whip the cream and add to the mixture. Leave to rest in the fridge for 20 minutes.

4. Meanwhile, roll out the pastry and use it to line a lightly greased 8 inch / 20 cm flan ring. Allow to rest in the fridge for 30 minutes, then line with foil and a layer of baking beans.

5. Bake in a moderate oven, Gas 6 /400°F / 200°C for about 25 minutes. Remove the foil and beans return to the oven for a further 10 minutes. Remove from the oven and allow to cool.

6. Whisk the filling again and pour the mixture into the flan case. Cook in a lowish oven, Gas 3 / 325°F / 170°C for about 1 1/2 hours.

7. Make the glaze by diluting the jam in a little hot water. Strain it and brush it over the cold tart using a soft pastry brush. Dust with icing sugar and serve

Chef's Tip: For some reason this recipe seems to make slightly more filling than necessary when made by different people. This is probably due to variations in technique. Although it grieves me to say it, discard any excess you may have left over!

Butterscotch Brulée

I truly think this is my all-time favourite dessert

Serves 6-8

Ingredients:
- 1 pint / 570 ml semi-skimmed milk
- 8 oz / 225 g soft dark brown sugar
- 8 oz / 225 g unsalted butter
- 4 oz / 110 g demerara or caster sugar (for the brulée)
- 2 medium-sized eggs
- 1 tbsp cornflour
- 1 vanilla pod (or a few drops of vanilla essence if not available)

6-8 x 3 inch / 7.5 cm diameter ramekins (6 oz / 175 g)

Method:

1. Boil the milk, and sugar and split vanilla pod in a thick-bottomed saucepan.

2. Whisk the eggs and cornflour together in a bowl and add the boiled milk.

3. Return the mixture back to the pan and bring to the boil. Strain into a bowl.

4. Cut the butter into pieces and whisk into the hot mixture.

5. Pour the mixture into the ramekins and leave to set overnight in the refrigerator.

6. Remove from the refrigerator and sprinkle with the demerara or caster sugar and glaze under a hot grill until the sugar caramelises.

7. Allow to cool and serve on small doilied plates.

Chef's Tip: To lighten the mixture add a quarter of a pint of lightly whipped cream before putting the mixture into the ramekins.

One day a restaurant customer ordered a dish he had never seen before - butterscotch brulée. It was quite the most delicious dessert he had ever tasted.

The next time he visited, he ordered it again. But the slightly embarrassed waiter told him that the item was off the menu that day.

A few days later the same thing happened. This time he insisted on seeing the chef to register his displeasure. The chef was most apologetic and promised that if the customer returned the next day he could have as many butterscotch brulées as he liked.

The customer did return, and got his just desserts, as you might say. He asked to see the chef to pass on his compliments, only to be told that it was his day off.

You see, I have always been addicted to butterscotch. And every morning, once the mixture had cooled, I was devouring the brulées while preparing for lunchtime service. The only way the customer could get a look-in was to turn up on my day off!

December

December took the leaf and walked with Al into the wood.

He reached down, and pulled back the snow from the ground, just as if it were a blanket. There lay Al's father, sleeping like a child. Al made up a meal from the left-over fish, and held it under his father's nose.

His father woke, and there, in the dead of winter they were reunited over a Christmas meal. And to this day Christmas is a time for joyous family reunion.

But when Al looked round to thank the months, there was nothing to be seen but the glowing embers of a bonfire.

Jerusalem Artichoke Soup

A smooth and nourishing soup for the heart of winter

Serves 4

Ingredients:

1 lb / 450 g Jerusalem artichokes, peeled and chopped
2 oz / 50 g onions, peeled and chopped
1 clove garlic, peeled
2 pts / 1.2 l chicken or vegetable stock (see pages 117 / 120)
2 oz / 50 g unsalted butter
1 oz / 25 g plain flour
¼ pt / 150 ml double cream
salt

Method:

1. Heat the butter in a thick-bottomed pan, and cook the onion and garlic for about 5 minutes without colouring.

2. Add the flour and continue to cook gently on a low heat for about 5 more minutes without colouring.

3. Gradually add the warmed stock, and bring to the boil. Add the artichokes and simmer for about 30 minutes. Liquidise and pass through a fine strainer into a clean pan.

4. Bring back to the boil, skim any fat from the top, adjust consistency with a little hot water if necessary, and season to taste.

5. Pour the soup into warm soup bowls, and add a swirl of cream to the top of each one. Serve immediately.

Well, here we are in December, the month of Christmas. So I thought I'd bring you a recipe from the Holy Land. There are only two problems with this: 1. I think it should be something to do with Bethlehem at this time of year, not Jerusalem, and 2. Even if it were to do with Jerusalem, I have never been able to work out what connection Jerusalem artichokes have with that city.

In fact, there is probably no vegetable in the world that has a greater identity crisis than the Jerusalem artichoke. In French, they are called Topinambours, which is the name of a Brazilian tribe. But this clue is just another ancestral dead end, as the vegetable is known to have originated in North America!

Jerusalem artichokes are tubers, like potatoes. They are in season from winter through to spring and their flavour is similar to that of real artichokes. They are quite knobbly and difficult to peel, like ginger. But if you make the effort I'm sure you will find the taste of this soup ample reward.

Scallops & Bacon with Honey & Sesame

A novel combination of flavours from land and sea

When Champagne Charlie was at Oxford, his father gave him a strict allowance:

When he first went up, he stayed with his Aunt Queenie. He had a great time at Oxford, where he formed his Champagne and Oyster habit. But amazingly, he never got into financial difficulties. Whenever his bank statements arrived, he flung them, unopened, into the bin.

But once a friend noticed the envelope, and pointed out that it had been steamed open and resealed. Charlie ripped it open. It showed a staggering sum bleeding from his account, compensated by a generous credit at the end of each month.

Aunt Queenie had enjoyed herself at university. Now she was reliving those days through the stories her profligate nephew told her of university life - and showing her gratitude in no uncertain terms! Perhaps you could use queen scallops for this recipe in her memory.

Serves 4 as a starter

Ingredients:

12 large scallops,
   1 oz / 15 g each, cleaned and trimmed
6 oz / 175 g smoked streaky bacon, cut into lardons
   (strips measuring 1 inch / 2.5 cm by $1/4$ inch / 5 mm)
4 oz / 110 g clear honey
1 tbsp toasted sesame seeds
juice of half a lemon
sesame oil for cooking
salt and milled pepper

Method:

1. Blanch the lardons in boiling water for 3 minutes, then refresh them under cold water. Drain them, and fry in a little hot sesame oil until crisp. Keep warm.

2. Heat a little sesame oil in a clean pan until almost smoking. Season the scallops lightly, and sear them in the hot oil for about $1 1/2$ minutes on each side, until they are nicely browned.

3. Remove the scallops from the pan and keep warm. Add the honey and lemon juice to the pan, and bring to the boil. Season to taste.

4. Place the scallops on warm plates. Pour the honey sauce over them, sprinkle with the lardons and sesame seeds. Garnish with a little tossed salad and serve.

Chef's Tip: Use only very fresh scallops, and do not overcook them!

Roast Suprême of Pheasant "Grande-Mère"

If you can't get poached pheasant, try and get it from your butcher, hung for between three days and two weeks

Serves 2

Ingredients:

- 1 young pheasant, plucked and prepared for roasting
- 3 oz / 75 g button onions
- 2 oz / 50 g button mushrooms
- 2 oz / 50 g smoked bacon lardons
- 1 slice thick white bread (cut into heart shaped croutons)
- 2 oz / 50 g unsalted butter
- 2 large glasses white wine (one for drinking during preparation!)
- $1/2$ pt / 275 ml chicken stock
- a few sprigs of fresh thyme

Method:

1. Prepare the pheasant for roasting, making sure that any shot is removed. Season with a little salt. Pre-heat the oven to a moderate heat Gas 7 / 425°F / 220°C.

2. Melt some butter in a casserole and brown the bird well on all sides. Transfer to the oven and cook for about 30 minutes, basting well. Remove from the oven.

3. Remove the bird from the casserole, retaining the juices and keep it warm.

4. Blanch the onions and lardons separately by placing them in cold water, bringing them to the boil and draining immediately.

5. Add the mushrooms, onions, thyme and lardons to the casserole and cook gently. Add the white wine and stock, and boil to reduce by half.

6. Fry the croutons in a little butter until golden brown.

7. Return the pheasant to the pan, cover and return to the oven for a further 10 minutes.

8. Remove from the oven, and carve the breasts onto plates, and serve with a little sauce and garnish, place the croutons on top. Keep the legs for a pâté or stew.

Champagne Charlie and I once rented a little cottage overlooking a village square in the Dordogne. One day, waking from an afternoon nap, I flung open the window to take the early night air. Suddenly the tranquillity was shattered by the clatter of two ancient bicycles. One was carrying Charlie. The other was carrying an elderly Frenchman!

In hot pursuit came another bike, carrying a gendarme. The three riders fetched up in a heap beneath my window. An animated discussion ensued, after which the the gendarme went on his way. Charlie came in and flung down a brace of pheasant. "Dinner for the weekend", he said. "Pheasant tastes better poached!"

"You've been poaching?" I asked, incredulously.

"With M. Magnanou, yes. 67 years old, and a finer poacher I have never met."

"But the gendarme caught you. Why aren't you locked up?"

"Gendarmes are only human Terry. They like pheasant as much as anyone. I imagine we shall have four for dinner at the weekend."

Roast Loin of Lamb Stuffed with Dried Exotic Fruits

A succulent festive dish with exotic Eastern overtones

Serves 6

I once read the autobiography of Tom Baker (ex-Dr Who). His real life has been almost as weird as that of a Time Lord. I suspect he is now working as a postman as I am sure I can discern the workings of a Time Lord in the postal service. Particularly around Christmas time.

For example, on Friends Restaurant's fifth birthday, we received a Christmas card congratulating us on our opening and wishing us all the best for the future. That was really spooky. The postmark showed it had been posted on our birthday five years earlier!

So I am playing my own time trick in this chapter. I haven't mentioned turkey, which is a relatively recent Victorian affectation. Instead I give you this main course for your festive table.

And if Dr Who is reading this, would he please tell his friends on the planet Gallifrey that I haven't received their Christmas Pudding orders yet. At this rate they won't get them until the year 3000. Particularly with retired Time Lords running the post!

Ingredients:

1½ lb / 675 g boneless loin of lamb, the skin still on in one piece, with the two loins trimmed of excess fat and sinews.
4 oz / 110 g chicken breast, skinned and boned
1 egg white
2 fl oz / 50 ml double cream
4 oz / 110 g (combined weight) dried exotic fruits such as mango, paw paw, kiwi fruit, apricots,
salt and pepper

Method:

1. Blend the chicken in a food processor. Add the egg white and blend until smooth. Turn the mixture out into a bowl, and gradually beat in the cream. Season lightly.

2. Chop the dried fruits into ¼ inch dice, and add to the mixture.

3. Lay the lamb out on a clean surface, skin side down. Season lightly and spread the mixture evenly over the meat.

4. Roll the meat neatly, and tie securely with string. Be careful not to force the stuffing out. Allow to rest in a cool place for 30 minutes.

5. Season the joint all over, and roast in a hot oven for about 55 minutes. Baste well during cooking.

6. When the meat is cooked, allow to rest for 20 minutes before carving. Insert a skewer through the centre, to test if the stuffing is cooked. If the juices run out clear, it is.

7. Carve the meat onto warm plates and serve with a little Red Wine Sauce (see page 117).

Chef's Tip: For a little extra flavour, de-glaze the roasting tray. Discard the fat, add ¼ pt / 150 ml water and the sauce, and boil for about 5 minutes, stirring with a wooden spoon to incorporate the sediment from the bottom of the pan.

Honey & Walnut Flan

A very tasty dessert, although I cannot vouch for its analgesic powers!

Serves 8

Ingredients:

    8 oz / 225 g walnuts
    5 oz / 150 g clear honey
    2 oz / 50 g caster sugar
    1 dsp of cornflour
    4 egg yolks
    1/2 pt / 275 ml double cream
    a few drops of vanilla essence
    1 lb / 450 g sweet pastry (see page 124)

Method:

1. Warm the honey and drop in the walnuts to soak for 2 1/2 hours.

2. Roll out the pastry and use it to line a lightly greased 8 inch / 20 cm flan ring. Allow to rest in the refrigerator for about 30 minutes.

3. Line the flan case with foil and a layer of baking beans to keep the base flat. Bake blind in a moderate oven, Gas 7 / 425°F / 220°C for 25 minutes. Remove the foil and beans and return to the oven for another 10 minutes.

4. Remove the walnuts from the honey and place them evenly in the bottom of the flan.

5. Whisk together the yolks, cornflour, sugar, cream and vanilla essence, and pour the mixture into the flan.

6. Bake in a moderate oven Gas 5 / 375°F / 190°C for about 50 minutes until lightly coloured. A skewer inserted carefully will come out clean when it is ready.

7. Boil the remaining honey, and strain into a bowl. When the flan is cool, glaze the top carefully with the honey, using a soft brush.

Chef's Tip: For a healthier option, substitute low fat yoghurt for half the cream.

Once on holiday I had been talking to the fishermen in the village pubs (as I usually do), and getting local recipe ideas from them. This one came from Harry, whose wife makes the best version of this tart in the world (in the completely unbiased view of her husband!)

We were discussing the recipe, and I told him that the ancient Greeks had been fascinated by walnuts, because of their resemblance to the human brain. They used to advocate eating walnuts as a cure for the inevitable post-Bacchanalian sufferings!

Harry looked at the recipe again. "In that case," he said this should be the ideal cure for me after drinking this local brew. It's just like treacle. I bet my brain is swimming around in it just like walnuts in honey!

With that, he got up to go staggering home. And I just hope poor Mrs Harry didn't have to get up too early in the morning to make her husband's hangover cure!

Chestnut Charlotte

A luxurious dessert to bring grace and flavour to the festive table

Serves 8

I once read the autobiography of Tom Baker (ex Dr Who) his real life has been almost as weird as that of the Time Lord. I suspect he is now working as a postman as I am sure I can discern the workings of a Time Lord in the postal service. Particularly around Christmas time. For example, on Friends Restaurant's fifth birthday, we received a Christmas card congratulating us on our opening and wishing us all the best for the future. That was really spooky. The postmark showed it had been posted on our birthday five years earlier!

So I am playing my own time trick in this chapter. i haven't mentioned turkey, which is a relatively recent Victorian affectation. Instead I give you this main course for your festive table.

And if Dr Who is reading this, would he please tell his friends on the planet Gallifrey that I haven't received their Christmas Pudding orders yet. At this rate they won't get them until the year 3000. Particularly with the retired Time Lords running the post !

Ingredients:

For the Bavarois:
1/2 pt / 275 ml milk
2 large eggs, separated
2 oz / 50 g caster sugar
1/2 oz / 15 g leaf gelatine
2 oz / 50 g sweetened chestnut purée
a few drops of vanilla essence
1/2 pt / 275 ml double cream
20-30 sponge fingers
8 marrons glacés (sweet glazed chestnuts)

For the Sponge Fingers:
4 eggs, separated
4 oz / 110 g plain flour
4 oz / 110 g caster sugar
a few drops of vanilla essence
icing sugar to finish

Method:

1. Soak the gelatine in cold water.

2. Whisk the yolks, sugar and vanilla together. Boil the milk and add gradually to the eggs, whisking continuously.

3. Return to the heat and cook gently until the mixture coats the back of a wooden spoon. Do not allow the mixture to boil.

4. Remove from the heat, add the drained gelatine, Stirring until completely dissolved, and strain into a bowl and allow to cool, without setting.

5. Meanwhile, line the charlotte mould with sponge fingers.

6. Whisk half the cream until it forms soft peaks and fold into the mixture. Whisk the egg whites until they form stiff peaks, and carefully fold them into the mixture also.

7. Carefully pour the mixture into the mould so as not to disturb the sponge fingers. Allow to set overnight.

8. Beat the remaining cream until stiff. Turn the charlotte out onto a serving dish and decorate with the cream. Garnish with the marrons glacés.

Chef's Tip: You must make your own sponge fingers for this recipe, as packet varieties tend to be too crisp.

The Sponge Fingers:

1. Cream the yolks, vanilla and sugar together thoroughly until white.

2. Whisk the egg whites until stiff. Gradually fold in portions of egg white alternately with sifting in portions of flour. (This must be carried out delicately to ensure lightness).

3. Pipe the mixture through a plain piping tube onto a baking tray lined with cooking parchment (silicone paper). Dust with icing sugar and allow to rest for a few minutes.

4. Bake in a moderate oven, Gas 6 / 400°F / 200°C for about 10 minutes.

Beurre Blanc (Butter Sauce)

Quantity: 1/2 pint / 300 ml

Ingredients:
- 2 oz / 50 g shallots, finely chopped
- 1 fl oz / 25 ml white wine vinegar
- 1 fl oz / 25 ml dry white wine
- 2 sprigs fresh thyme
- 1 tsp crushed peppercorns
- 1 fl oz / 25 ml double cream
- 5 oz / 150 g unsalted butter, cut into small cubes
- a few drops of lemon juice

When using butter to make or enrich sauces, use chilled butter straight from the fridge, cut into small dice. This makes it easier to incorporate.

Method:

1. Place the shallots, wine, vinegar and peppercorns in a pan over a gentle heat and reduce until almost dry.

2. Add the cream and bring to the boil.

3. Turn the heat down low and add the butter gradually, shaking the pan gently, or whisking until completely combined.

4. Strain the sauce into a clean pan, add the lemon juice and season.

Basic Recipes - Sauces

Red Wine Sauce

Quantity: ½ pint / 300 ml

Ingredients:
    2 pts / 1.2 l veal or beef stock,
      reduced by half by simmering for about 30 minutes
    4 oz / 110 g shallots, roughly chopped
    2 cloves garlic, smashed
    2 sprigs fresh thyme
    ¼ pt / 150 ml red wine
    2 oz / 50 g unsalted butter

When reducing sauces or stock, do so gently and without boiling too rapidly, as this can cause a bitter taste to develop or even burn the ingredients.

Method:
1. Melt the butter in a thick-bottomed pan and gently cook the shallots and garlic, allowing to colour slightly.
2. Add the wine and herbs, bring to the boil and reduce by half.
3. Add the stock and reduce very gently by half again.
4. Pass the sauce through a fine sieve or strainer and use as required.

Chicken Stock

Quantity: 2 pints / 1.2 l

Ingredients:

    1 1/2 lb / 675 g chicken bones
    8 oz / 225 g onions, celery and carrots,
      peeled and roughly chopped
    1 bay leaf
    1 sprig fresh thyme
    a few parsley stalks

Method:

1. Place the raw bones in a stockpot or large saucepan and cover with cold water.

2. Bring to the boil and skim off any fat.

3. Add the vegetables and herbs, bring back to the boil and simmer gently for about 2 hours. Skim the surface regularly and top up with water as necessary.

4. Pass the stock through a fine sieve or strainer and use as required.

When making stocks, it is important to top up periodically with cold water, thereby allowing fat to rise to the surface and rendering it easy to skim off.

Basic Recipes - Stocks

Fish Stock

Quantity: 2 pints / 1.2 l

Ingredients:
    2 lb / 900 g white fish bones (sole is best)
    3 oz / 75 g finely sliced onions
    juice of half a lemon
    1 bay leaf
    1 small sprig fresh thyme
    a few parsley stalks

Do not overcook fish stock, as it will become oily, and lose it's fresh taste.

Method:

1. Wash the bones and place them in a large saucepan. Cover with cold water and bring to the boil.

2. Skim the surface and add the onions and herbs. Add the lemon juice and simmer for 20 minutes.

3. Skim and pass the stock through a fine sieve or strainer and use as required.

Veal or Beef Stock

Quantity: 2 pts / 1.2 l

Ingredients:
- 2 lb / 900 g veal or beef bones
- 8 oz / 225 g onions, celery and carrots, peeled and roughly chopped
- 1 large bay leaf
- 1 good sprig fresh thyme
- 2 tbsp tomato purée

Method:

1. Roast the bones in a hot oven until nicely browned, then place them in a stockpot or large saucepan and cover with cold water.

2. Place the vegetables in the roasting tray and brown them, either in the oven or on a gas ring, then discard any fat from the roasting tray, and de-glaze by adding water and simmering for a few minutes, stirring to incorporate the sediment from the bottom of the pan. Add the tomato purée and the herbs and combine well.

3. Tip this into the stockpot, bring to the boil and simmer for about 8 hours, skimming the surface from time to time and topping up with water as necessary.

4. Strain through a fine sieve or strainer and use as necessary.

Always bring stock to the boil and then simmer slowly. Rapid boiling will cloud the stock and distribute undesirable fat throughout the liquid.

Basic Recipes - Stocks

Vegetable Stock

Quantity: 2 pts / 1.2 l

Ingredients:

12 oz / 350 g onions, celery, leeks and carrots,
   peeled and roughly chopped
2 cloves garlic, smashed
1 large bay leaf
2 sprigs fresh thyme
a few parsley stalks
6 crushed peppercorns

Method:

1   Place all the ingredients in a stockpot or large saucepan and cover with cold water.

2   Bring to the boil and simmer for about 1 hour, skimming the surface pregularly and topping up with water as necessary.

3   Pass the stock through a fine sieve or strainer and use as required.

For recipes requiring a darker colour, add 1 tbsp tomato purée at stage 1.

Crème Anglaise

Quantity: 1/2 pint / 275 ml

Ingredients:
- 1/2 pint / 275 ml milk
- 3 egg yolks
- 1 vanilla pod, split lengthways down the middle
- 1 1/2 oz / 40 g caster sugar

Method:

1. Place the vanilla pod in the milk and bring to the boil. Remove from the heat and allow to infuse for a few minutes.

2. Whisk the egg yolks and sugar together in a bowl, and then add the hot milk gradually, whisking continuously.

3. Return the pan to a low heat and cook gently, stirring continuously until the sauce coats the back of a wooden spoon. Do not allow to boil otherwise the eggs will scramble and ruin the sauce.

   Chef's Tip: Put half the sugar in the milk when first bringing it to the boil to help prevent it from burning.

When using eggs in sauces, they must be cooked at a reasonably high temperature, but not so high that the egg proteins denature, as happens when eggs are boiled or scrambled. The usual way to test whether and egg-based sauce, such as créme anglaise, is cooked, is to coat the back of a wooden spoon.

Basic Recipes - Pastry

Raspberry Coulis

When making fruit coulis, a few drops of lemon juice will enhance and help bring out the fruit flavour.

Quantity: 1/2 pint / 275 ml

Ingredients:
1 lb / 450 g raspberries (preferable fresh, but frozen will do)
5 oz / 150 g caster sugar
1/4 pt / 150 ml water
A few drops of lemon juice

Method:

1. Bring the water and sugar to the boil and add the raspberries.

2. Remove from the heat and allow to infuse until cold.

3. Liquidise and pass through a fine strainer, forcing as much of the pulp through as possible.

4. Add a few drops of lemon juice to taste, and adjust the consistency with a little water if necessary.

Chef's Tip: Add a little liqueur to the coulis, according to the dish it is required to accompany.

NB: For strawberry coulis substitute the raspberries for the strawberries.

Frangipane

Quantity: 12 oz / 350 g

Ingredients:
- 4 oz / 110 g butter
- 4 oz / 110 g caster sugar
- 4 oz / 110 g ground almonds
- 1/2 oz / 10 g flour
- 2 eggs

Method:

1. Cream the butter and sugar together in a food processor. Add the eggs gradually until a smooth consistency is achieved.

2. Mix in the almonds and flour gently. Do not beat the mixture - simply fold the ingredients in. Leave to rest for 30 minutes.

Basic Recipes - Pastry

Sweet Pastry

Quantity: 12 oz / 350 g

Ingredients:
- 8 oz / 225 g plain flour
- 2 oz / 50 g caster sugar
- 4 oz /110 g butter
- 1 egg
- a few drops of vanilla essence

Method:

1. Blend the butter and flour in a food processor to achieve a breadcrumb texture.

2. Whisk the egg, sugar and vanilla essence together and add gradually to the mixture.

3. Blend the resulting mixture until smooth. Leave to rest for 1 hour in the fridge.

Shortcrust Pastry

Quantity: 12 oz / 350 g

Ingredients:

    8 oz / 225 g plain flour
    4 oz / 110 g cold, unsalted butter, cut into cubes
    1/2 cup cold water
    pinch of salt
    1 tsp icing sugar
    a few drops of lemon juice

Method:

1. Sieve the flour, sugar and salt into a bowl.

2. Rub the butter into the flour, using your thumbs and forefingers, lifting them above the bowl to aerate the mixture, until you achieve the consistency of breadcrumbs.

3. Add the lemon juice to the water and gradually mix in using a fork. Add just enough to form a firm dough.

4. Turn out onto a lightly floured work surface, and gently shape into a ball. Do not overwork the pastry as this could render the dough tough. Wrap in clingfilm and allow to rest in a cool place for 30 minutes before use.

NB: The use of icing sugar adds to the shortness of the pastry, but the quantity is insufficient to sweeten the dough.

Basic Recipes - Pastry

Suet Pastry

Quantity: 12 oz / 350 g

Ingredients:
- 8 oz / 225 g plain flour
- 4 oz / 110 g suet, beef or vegetarian
- 1 tsp baking powder
- 3 fl oz / 75 ml cold water
- pinch of salt

Method:

1. Sift the flour, baking powder and salt into a bowl.

2. Rub in the suet until it has the consistency of breadcrumbs.

3. Make a well in the centre, and gradually add the water.

4. Knead the mixture to a smooth dough, taking care not to over work it or it may become tough.

5. Wrap in cling film and leave to rest for 30 minutes, or until required.

Glossary

Bavarois	A cold dessert, made from egg custard, set with gelatine and lightened with whipped cream
Bain-Marie	A container of water, used for cooking in the oven, without burning a roasting tray would suffice
Beurre Blanc	A butter sauce.
Compote	Stewed fruits, sometimes refers to vegetables
Croutons	Fried or toasted bread, in various shapes, ie. dice, hearts and flutes (cut from baguettes)
Dariole	Mould, as those used in making Crème Caramel
De-glaze	Term used for incorporating the sediment left in a pan, after roasting or frying, by adding wine, water, or stock, and simmering whilst stirring, to enrich a gravy or sauce.
Egg wash	Beaten egg, used for sealing or glazing pastry
Flan	An open tart.
Galette	A savoury pancake, or term sometimes used to describe a pancake-like dish.
Gelatine	A soluble protein used to set food.
Lardons	Streaky bacon cut into thick strips.
Marinate	To immerse in a herbed or spiced liquid, in order to impart flavour.
Mousse	A dish of light consistency.
Noisette	Normally cut from a boneless loin of lamb, but now applied to other meats and fish
Polenta	A solid or creamy paste made from cornmeal, used to accompany dishes, (Italian)
Sauté	To cook in a pan or frying pan, using oil or butter.
Suprême	Normally refers to the breast of poultry, but can now apply to a centre cut of fish fillet,
Seal	To colour or seal the outside of meat or fish, in a pan or the oven, in order to seal in the juices.
Terrine	A dish, normally in the shape of a bread tin, used for making pâtés, etc. sometimes refers to a dish which has been prepared in one
Quenelle	The shape made by using 2 spoons, usually from a mousse or pâté.

Index

Apple and Calvados Tart	49
Asparagus	28
Aubergines, Galette of	20
Avocado and Smoked Chicken	67
Black Noodles	85
Brandade, Bulwinkle's	45
Breast of Pigeon	9
Bubble and Squeak	32
Butterscotch Brulée	107
Calves Liver	32
Caramelised Onion Tart	38
Chestnut Charlotte	116
Chicken Breast, Poached	17
Chicken, Jambonneau of	57
Chicken in Ratatouille	75
Chocolate Marquise	41
Chocolate Soufflé	35
Clafoutis	89
Coconut Parfait	64
Confit of Duck	40
Courgette Soufflé	15
Crab Cakes	66
Crabmeat Sausage	81
Date and Banana Pudding	24
Duck Livers	44
Emmental	38
Exotic Fruits	112
Fennel	98
Fig	100
Fillet of Beef	33
Fishcakes	29
Garlic Mash	40
Gnocchi Spinach	104
Goats' Cheese and Red Pepper Tart	73
Grape Tart	21
Green Bean and Tarragon Soup	80
Grilled Goats Cheese with Celery and Walnuts	103
Grilled Salmon	10
Guinea Fowl	46
Halibut	85
Honey	12
Honey & Walnut Flan	113
Jerusalem Artichoke, soup	109
Kipper Pâté	102
Lamb, Loin of	112
Lardons	9
Lemon Pudding Soufflé	13
Lime Tart	106
Lobster	93
Mackerel	45
Marinated Salmon	37
Meringue, Hazelnut	99
Mille-Feuille	70
Mushrooms	33,39,60
Monkfish, Roast	60
Orange Bread and Butter Pudding	48
Pancakes, Smoked Salmon	16
Partridge Pudding	97
Pear and Almond Tart	42
Pheasant	111
Pigeon	9
Polenta	39
Pork, Noisettes of	69
Prune and Armagnac Tart	34
Raspberry Mille-Feuille	70
Rhubarb Tart Brulée	61
Rillettes of Duck	53
Roast Loin of Lamb	112
Rösti	84
Salmis of Wild Duck	105
Salmon Baked in Filo	47
Salmon Fishcakes	29
Scallops and Bacon	110
Sea Bass	98
Sea Fish	8
Smoked Chicken	67
Smoked Salmon Pancakes	16
Sole, Terrine of Lobster and,	93
Soused Herrings	74
Spätzle	11
Spinach	9
Spinach Gnocchi	104
Strawberry Délice	78
Strudel, Vegetable	76
Summer Pudding	88
Suprême of Pheasant	111
Terrine of Lobster and Sole	93
Terrine of Seafish	8
Tuna	68
Vegetable Strudel	76
Venison Stew	11
Vermouth	85
Vichysoisse	96
Victoria Plum and Amaretti Tart	77
Warm Fig and Wild Honey Tart	100
Watercress Soup	56
White Chocolate Bavarois	71
Wild Boar Medallions and Rösti	84
Wild Duck	105
Wild Mushrooms	33,60